John Shortall Macaulay

Treatise on Field Fortification

The Attack of Fortresses, Military Mining and Reconnoitring. Second Edition

John Shortall Macaulay

Treatise on Field Fortification
The Attack of Fortresses, Military Mining and Reconnoitring. Second Edition

ISBN/EAN: 9783337267322

Printed in Europe, USA, Canada, Australia, Japan

Cover: Foto ©Paul-Georg Meister /pixelio.de

More available books at **www.hansebooks.com**

PREFACE TO SECOND EDITION.

THE original manuscript of this little work was carefully criticised by the late Sir John Jones, Bart., Major-General in the Corps of Royal Engineers. To that criticism the compiler attributes the favourable reception it has received from the public, and he takes the opportunity offered by the publication of a second edition to acknowledge his obligations to that distinguished officer.

18*th* Nov., 1847.

PREFACE TO FOURTH EDITION.

The arrangement of this Treatise has been altered considerably, and additions have been made to it, in accordance with the advice of Captain Bainbrigge, Royal Engineers, Professor of Fortification at the Royal Military Academy at Woolwich, which it is hoped will render this edition more useful than the former ones.

It may be here remarked that as *every officer* ought to be well acquainted with the mode of fortifying an outpost, it may be advantageous for those who have not *time* to go through the whole volume regularly, to begin with the Eighth Chapter, which contains an account of that important subject, and then study the Ninth Chapter, in which the attack and defence of outposts are described.

TABLE OF CONTENTS.

[*.* Those dimensions on the Plates which have no marks attached, denote yards; feet are marked ', inches"—so, in Figure 1, 4' 3" is to be read 4 feet 3 inches.]

CHAPTER I.

Section I.

	Page
Introductory Observations	1

Section II.

	Page
Profile of Works	4
Penetration of Projectiles	6
Table of Width of Ditches	12

Section III.

	Page
Trace of Works	15
General Rules applicable to all Fortifications	15

Section IV.

	Page
Open Works	18
The Redan	18
The Lunette	20
The Double Redan	21

CONTENTS.

SECTION V.

	PAGE
ENCLOSED WORKS	22
Redoubts	22
Table of Minima of Redoubts	29
Star Forts	30
Demi-bastioned Forts	32
Bastioned Forts	33

CHAPTER II.

SECTION I.

THE OUTLINE OF FIELD WORKS CONSIDERED IN COMBINATION WITH EACH OTHER	38
Continued Lines	38
Redan Lines	41
Continued Redan Lines	42
Tenaille Line	43
Indented Lines	44
Bastioned Lines	45

SECTION II.

LINES WITH INTERVALS	48

CHAPTER III.

SECTION I.

EXECUTION OF THE WORKS	55
Profiling	55
Division of Labour	58

SECTION II.

REVETMENTS	63
Parapet Revetment	63

CONTENTS.

	PAGE
Fascine Revetment	63
Hurdle Revetment	67
Sod Revetment	68
Plank and Cask Revetments	70
Gabion Revetment	70
Revetment of Sand-bags	72
Scarp Revetments	73

CHAPTER IV.

OF THE DETAILS.

SECTION I.

BARBETTES AND TRAVERSES, &c.	75
Passages	79
Bridges at the Entrances	80
Powder Magazines	82
Embrasures	84
Platforms	86
Barriers	87
Chevaux-de-Frise	82

SECTION II.

OBSTACLES	89
Abattis	91
Military Pits	92
Inundations	93
Pickets	95
Crows' feet	96
Palisades and Fraises	97

SECTION III.

DEFENCE OF THE DITCH	100

CONTENTS.

	PAGE
Stockades	100
Kaponiers	100
Counterscarp Galleries	102

Section IV.

INTERIOR INTRENCHMENTS	103
Defensible Barracks	103
Loop-holes	106

CHAPTER V.

Section I.

ON THE MANNER OF OCCUPYING IRREGULAR SITES	108
Scarped Slopes	109
Parapets on Sloping Ground	113
Parapets on Steep Slopes	115

Section II.

ON DEFILADE	115
Objects of	115
Practical Methods of Defilading Field-works	118
Method of Determining the Height of Traverses	122
Defilade of Lines	124

CHAPTER VI.

DEFENCE OF RIVERS AND WATER-COURSES.

Section I.

OF BRIDGE-HEADS	126
Security of the Banks of Rivers	131

CONTENTS.

SECTION II.

	PAGE
OF INUNDATIONS AND DAMS	134
Profile of Dams	135
Construction of Waste Weir	137
Sluice-gates	139
To calculate the Produce of a Stream	140

CHAPTER VII.

PASSAGE OF RIVERS	142
Military Bridges	145
Weight of Men, Horses, and 12-pounders	146
Carts or Waggons to form Bridges	148
Flying and Raft Bridges	149
Cask and Trestle Bridges	150
Pontoon Bridges	150

CHAPTER VIII.

MILITARY POSTS, AND WORKS THROWN UP ON THE EVE OF BATTLE	152
Mode of Preparing Hedges for Defence	157
Mode of Preparing Walls for Defence	159
Tambours to flank Walls	160
Mode of fortifying Churches and other Large Buildings	163
Machicoulis Gallery	164
Substitute for Machicoulis Gallery	165
Blindages	166
Farm or Country-houses, to fortify	167
Block-houses	169
Block-houses to resist Artillery	171
Economical Mode of constructing a Block-house	172

CHAPTER IX.

ON THE DEFENCE AND ATTACK OF FIELD-WORKS AND MILITARY POSTS.

	PAGE
ON THE DEFENCE	174
To guard and defend an Earthen Work	175
To guard and defend a Church or other Building	179
Manner of guarding and defending an Intrenched Village	180
ON THE ATTACK	184
Attacks by Surprise	185
Attacks by Stratagem	192
Attacks by Open Force	192
Attack of Fortified Buildings	195

CHAPTER X.

MILITARY MINING.

Dimensions of Galleries and Branches	199
On those now used at Chatham	200
Construction of Shafts	201
To find the Length of the Intervals of Shafts	202
To sink Shafts	203
Construction of Galleries	205
Returns in Galleries	207
To find the Length of the Intervals of Galleries	209
Branch Galleries lined with Cases	211
Shafts *a la Boule*	212
Of Mine Chambers	213
To place the Hose-Troughs	215
Common Mines	217
Charges of Common Mines	220
Do. Globes of Compression	222
Do. Undercharged Mines	223

CONTENTS. xiii

	PAGE
Tamping of Mines	223
Manner of firing Mines	224
Manner of Using the Monk	225
The Rocket	226
Firing Mines by Voltaic Electricity	228
Blasts	231
Demolitions	234
To breach a Wall	234
To breach a Wall supporting a Terrace	234
Demolition of Revetments	235
Demolition of a Tower	237
Demolition of a Powder-magazine	238
Demolition of Bridges	239
Demolition of a House	240
Of Fougasses	241
Of Shell Fougasses	241
Of Stone Fougasses	243

CHAPTER XI.

ATTACK OF FORTRESSES.

General Description	245
Working Parties, and Materials for Batteries, &c.	261

CHAPTER XII.

MILITARY RECONNOISSANCE	265

APPENDIX.

Note I. On Defilade	307
Note II. On Mining	329
Note III. Do.	331
Note IV. Do.	334
Note V. Do.	336

FIELD FORTIFICATION.

CHAPTER I.

SECTION I.

INTRODUCTORY OBSERVATIONS.

1. FORTIFICATION may be considered as both natural and artificial—rocks, rivers, mountains, &c., being natural fortifications.

Artificial fortification consists in improving the obstacles presented by nature, or in forming them where wanting, so that the troops occupying a fortified position may be enabled to repel the assaults of a much superior force. During a campaign, an army seldom occupies any particular tract of country for a long period; the fortifications thrown up for the defence of positions, under such circumstances, are in general hastily executed, with more or less stability according to the nature of the means available, and the time allowed for their completion; in most cases they are formed of earth only, and are called *Intrenchments*.

2. When works are constructed in a solid and durable manner, and intended to exist many years, they are termed *Permanent Fortifications*, whilst those which are only wanted for periods not exceeding one or two campaigns, perhaps only for a few days, are termed *Field Fortifications*. In permanent fortification every means required for rendering the works substantial and perfect is supposed to be provided: while in the field, on the contrary, even those most necessary are often wanting, and it is in such cases that an officer has an opportunity of shewing his activity and resources, as well as his foresight and patience; he should know how to apply the means in his power to the greatest advantage, how to induce the soldiers and labourers under his orders to work vigorously, without exacting too much from them; he should carefully avoid giving contradictory orders, and not lose sight of the main object by attaching himself to trifling minutiæ; he should always be the first on the ground, and the last to leave it, and should not disdain using the tools of the workmen to instruct them in the best mode of handling them.

3. If troops were not sufficiently powerful to manœuvre in the field, they would endeavour to interpose impediments to the progress of their enemies, to obtain cover from the effects of their weapons, and to secure the means of using their own with the greatest advantage.

For this purpose existing obstacles may be taken advantage of, but a ditch is usually dug to impede the enemy's progress, the earth excavated therefrom is thrown to the rear and formed into bank or mask, behind which the defenders, no longer exposed to the view of the enemy, are greatly protected from the effects of his weapons, and such a form is given to the bank as will enable them, when required, to use their own with full effect.

The mass of earth thus thrown up by the defenders for their protection is called a *parapet*.*

4. In order to represent upon paper the works used in fortification, plans, elevations, and sections are required.

The *plan* represents objects as seen from above and projected on a horizontal plane.

The *elevation* shews the projection of the surface of an object on a vertical plane.

The *section* shews the form of the intersection of a work by a vertical plane; and if the plane is at right angles to the general direction of the work, the section is called a *profile*.

* *It. para petto*, guard the breast.

SECTION II.

ON THE PROFILE OF WORKS.

5. The *plane of site* of a work is a plane representing the general direction of the surface of the ground on which it stands.

The *relief* of a work is the height of its highest point above the bottom of the ditch; the *command* is its height above a point in the plane of site directly below it.

6. The parapet should always be of sufficient height to screen the defenders from the fire of the enemy, whence it follows that the command of a parapet on level ground, viz., AB in the profile, Fig 1, ought not to be less than $6\frac{1}{2}$ feet; and this height is only applicable to unimportant works, for as the lines of flight of missiles are often much curved, troops could only be secure from their effects when placed *close* to parapets of that height; also if only $6\frac{1}{2}$ feet of command were given to the parapet, the men mounted on the banquettes of the rear face of a work would not be covered from the view of the enemy in front, unless the interior space were of great extent.

These considerations have induced engineers to prescribe 8 feet as the proper command for intrenchments on level ground.

However considerable this command may appear for field-works, it is not sufficient in all cases to protect the men mounted on the banquettes from *enfilade, slant,** or *reverse fire*. It may here be proper to define the terms just used.

Enfilade fire is that which is parallel, or nearly so, to the crest of the parapet; slant fire, that which strikes the exterior of the parapet obliquely; reverse fire, that which strikes the interior slope of the parapet. In proportion as the height of the parapet is increased, the defect of being exposed to enfilade, slant, or reverse fire diminishes, but the fire from the parapet becomes at the same time more plunging.

Intrenchments constructed in haste have sometimes only a command of 5 feet. This height of parapet not being sufficient to cover a man of ordinary stature, a small trench must be dug in the rear, and a banquette formed with the earth excavated from it. The trench should be about 18 inches deep; a man may then stand upright in it, without exposing himself to the view of the enemy.

The dimensions adopted must be proportionate to the time and means available, and must be such *that the works may be defensible in the shortest time*, and that they may be easily strengthened, if time permit, by thickening the parapets.

**Fr.* En écharpe.

The *thickness* of the top of a parapet must be varied in proportion to the penetration of the projectiles it is intended to resist. It has been ascertained by experiment, that a musket-ball, at a mean range, buries itself nearly 1 foot 6 inches in common earth, dug up, and well rammed; that a ball from a

6-pounder buries itself from	$3\frac{1}{4}$ to $4\frac{1}{4}$	feet.
9 do.	$6\frac{1}{4}$ to 7	,,
12 do	$8\frac{1}{4}$ to 10	,,
18 and 24 do.	$11\frac{1}{4}$ to 13	,,

In order, therefore, that the enemy's shot may not penetrate much more than $\frac{2}{3}$ of the width of the parapet, it must have the following thicknesses.

For musket-balls	3 feet.
6-pound shot	6 ,,
9 do.	9 ,,
12 do.	13 ,,
18 and 24 do.	18 ,,

18 and 24-pounders are rarely carried into the field; the greatest thickness required for the parapet of a field-work is, consequently, 13 feet in general.

A small terrace, DEF, is formed along the interior of the parapet, excepting where artillery are to be placed, so that men may mount upon it, and fire over the parapet: this is the *banquette* or *footbank*, as it was termed formerly.

To allow for the mean height of a man, the distance of the *banquette* below the point A is usually made 4¼ feet, the height over which a man can conveniently fire.

The ramp, EF, conducting to the banquette, has usually a base, GF, equal to twice its height, EG, except when the parapet is much more than 8 feet high, and in this case the banquette is ascended by steps, with a rise of 9 inches, and a tread, or width, of 1 foot.

The *tread* of the banquette, DE, is made 3 feet wide when the parapet is to be defended by a single rank, and 4½ feet wide for double rank, having a slope of 2 inches to the rear to carry off the rain.

The top AI of the parapet has a *superior slope* so directed that the defenders when mounted on the banquette may see the exterior edge of the ditch. This slope is a necessary evil,—an evil, because the less the inclination of the superior slope the stronger will be the parapet; it should, therefore, never exceed ¼ ; (viz. IK should not be more than ¼ of AK) and it usually does not exceed ⅙.

The *interior slope*, AD, can seldom in the field be lined with brick or stone, or other material capable of maintaining itself without a slope; a base of from 1 to 1¼ feet is therefore given to this slope.

The *exterior slope*, IH, ought always to be left

at the natural slope of the earth; it varies therefore according to the nature of the ground, in ordinary cases not being much more or less than 45°. The intersection A of the superior and interior slopes is called the *crest* or *interior crest* [*] of the parapet, that of the superior and exterior slopes being the *exterior crest*.

The rear side of the ditch LN is called the *scarp*, and the outer side MO the *counterscarp*. The space HL is called the *berm;* it should generally not be made more than 1½ feet wide, that it may facilitate the escalading of the work as little as possible. It would, undoubtedly, be better on that account not to have a berm, but it cannot always be dispensed with, being often required to prevent the weight of the parapet breaking down the scarp, and thus to give greater stability to the work. The berm is usually left on the natural level of the ground; consequently, the enemy, when on it, is no longer exposed to the musketry fire of the parapet in its rear. If made less than 6 feet below the interior crest of the parapet, the defenders mounted on the banquette would have little advantage over an enemy on the berm.

The slopes of the scarp, and of the counterscarp, vary in inclination according to the nature of the earth, the means by which they are secured, and

[*] *Fr.* Crête intérieure, ligne couvrante, ou ligne de feu.

the degree of permanency desired. When required to stand the effects of the autumnal rains, or during a winter, and no means of retaining the earth can be procured, they must have the natural slope of the ground ; but if required for a short time only, they may be made ⅓ or ¼ ;* *i. e.* the base of the slope may be made equal to ⅓ or ¼ of its height,† according to the nature of the soil.

The counterscarp is generally made steeper than the scarp, because it has not to support the weight of the parapet.

The slopes of ditches, &c., may be made steeper in temperate than in cold climates, the frost in the latter doing more damage than the rain in the former.

* The inclination of each surface is usually represented by a *fraction* in which the denominator represents the length of the base, and the numerator the perpendicular of the triangle showing its profile.

† To apply a profile to the plan of the interior crest of the parapet, when the profile is everywhere the same, it is only necessary to draw parallels to the interior crest, through the several angles formed by the lines of a profile constructed perpendicular to the parapet, as in Fig. 2; and when the parapet forms a salient angle, the lines representing the bottom and top of the counterscarp are made circular, being described from the angle formed by the meeting of the scarp lines as a centre.

When the height of the parapet is greater at one end than at the other, a profile must be constructed at each end, and lines must then be drawn joining the corresponding points of each profile. The interior crest of the parapet is always represented by a thick line.

When the covering mass has no banquette it is called an *Epaulment*. The artillery make use of epaulments to cover their guns, and they are sometimes thrown up to protect cavalry from the enemy's fire during the time when their active services are not often required—as, for instance, when they are supporting the operations of a siege.

7. Though in some cases, as, for instance, in rocky situatious, the dimensions given to the parapet must depend upon the quantity of earth that can be procured from the ditch, yet generally the width and depth of the ditch are proportioned to the content of the parapet. It follows, then, that these dimensions must vary with the height and thickness of the latter.

The means provided for the execution of works in the field seldom permit of the ditches being made more than 12 feet deep. The depth of the ditches of field-works may, therefore, vary from $6\frac{1}{2}$ to 12 feet; and they should, if possible, be at least 13 feet wide at top.

8. In order to calculate the width and depth of a ditch, proportionate to the area of the profile of the parapet, attention should be paid to the fact that earth newly raised is increased in volume about $\frac{1}{10}$ or $\frac{1}{12}$.

Let S be the area of the profile of the parapet of any known dimensions; S' that of the profile of the ditch; C the length of the path of the centre of gravity, generated by the motion of the profile of the parapet along the interior crest; C′ the same line with reference to the profile of the ditch, and $\frac{1}{m}$ the increase of the volume of the earth by its removal.

The solid formed by the movement of a plane figure along a line being equal to the surface of the moveable figure multiplied by the distance traversed by its centre of gravity, we have the following relation between the parapet and ditch:—

$$C\ S = C'\ S' + \frac{C'S'}{m} \text{ and } C'\ S' = C\ S \times \frac{m}{m \times 1}$$

The first term given, the second depends on the form, or profile, of the ditch; of which it is evidently necessary to assume one dimension in order to obtain the others.

The depth, being a quantity contained within narrow limits, is the dimension commonly assumed as known.

The following table shows the width of ditches, required for the profiles of parapets most frequently adopted in field-works.

For the purpose of calculation it has been assumed—that the banquette is 4 feet 3 inches below the crest of the parapet, with a tread 3 feet wide, and a slope of 2 inches to the rear—that the base of the slope of the banquette is double its height; that of the interior slope being 1 foot— that the superior slope is at $\frac{1}{6}$ in the first nine profiles, and at ⅛ in the remainder—that the exterior slope is at 45°—that the seventh, eighth, and ninth profiles have a glacis 1 foot high, its interior slope being 45°, and superior slope $\frac{1}{15}$, and that the three following profiles have a similar glacis 2 feet high, the three next, one of 3 feet, and the last three, one of 4 feet in height. The * is to show that the sides of those ditches meet in a point in the profile. *(See Table.)*

Number of Profile.	KNOWN QUANTITIES.			WIDTH OF DITCHES.			
	Height of Parapet.	Thickness of Parapet.	Depth of Ditch.	Scarp is at ⅔ and Counterscarp at ⅘.	Scarp at ⅔ Counterscarp, at ¼.	Ccarp 45°, Counterscarp ⅐.	Scarp and Counterscarp 45°
	Feet.	Feet.	Feet.	Ft. In.	Ft. In.	Ft. In.	Ft. In.
1	6¼	6	8	10 5	11 5	*14 1	*16 1
2	...	9	9	11 3	12 3	*15 2	*17 6
3	...	14	10	12 3	13 7	*16 9	*19 4
4	8	6	12	11 7	13 7	*17 1	*19 8
5	...	9	...	13 0	14 5	18 5	*21 3
6	...	14	...	14 10	16 4	20 4	*23 4
7	9	6	...	14 5	16 0	20 0	*22 10
8	...	9	...	16 0	17 5	21 5	24 5
9	...	14	...	18 2	19 8	23 8	26 8
10	10	6	...	19 0	20 5	24 5	27 5
11	...	9	...	20 9	22 3	6 3	29 3
12	...	14	...	23 7	25 1	29 1	32 1
13	11	6	...	24 11	26 5	30 5	33 5
14	...	9	...	26 11	28 5	32 5	35 5
15	...	14	...	31 1	31 7	35 7	38 7
16	12	6	...	32 5	33 11	37 11	40 11
17	...	9	...	34 8	36 2	40 2	43 2
18	...	14	...	38 2	39 8	43 8	46 8

9. The width of the ditch may also be determined in the following manner. Divide the surface S of the profile of the parapet by the depth of the ditch, and this will give the width at the top; for instance, if the area of the parapet be 108 superficial feet, and the ditch is to be 6 feet deep, it must be 18 feet wide. This calculation supposes the ditch to be excavated with vertical sides, that the volume of the excavation is not increased, and that the distance traversed by the centres of gravity of the parapet and ditch are equal, none of which suppositions are correct; but it will be found that the increase caused by the slopes of the ditch when at $\frac{1}{1}$ is very nearly equivalent to the increase of volume of the excavation, and to the increase of length of the ditch; and that this rule will be sufficiently near the truth for practice in the field.

10. Although the parapets have been supposed not to be less than $6\frac{1}{2}$ feet high, when constructed on a plain, yet, in works of small importance, not required to cover any space in their rear, a less command may be given; but in no case should the command of a parapet be less than 5 feet; and then it would be necessary to lower the berm, in order that the enemy when on it might not see into the interior of the intrenchment.

The means of execution commonly available in the field, together with the great increase of labour consequent on the formation of parapets more than 8 feet high, necessarily prescribe a limit to that height, which on ordinary occasions should not be passed; this limit may be assumed at 12 feet.

In all works of slight profile, the scarp and counterscarp should be carried down to meet in a point; and unless means of securing these slopes are provided, or they are left at the natural slope of the ground, the ditch can seldom be made more than 12 feet deep, without endangering the stability of the work.

When parapets are made of more than common height, the superior slope cannot be directed on the edge of the counterscarp; a glacis, Fig. 25, should then be formed in front of the counterscarp, the crest of which must be kept at least $5\frac{1}{2}$ feet below that of the parapet.

In this case, also, the banquette should be ascended by steps, both to diminish as much as possible the quantity of excavation, and not to occupy too great a portion of the interior space.

The rise of each step should be from 9 inches to 1 foot, the tread from 1 to $1\frac{1}{2}$ feet wide, with an inclination towards the interior of the work, to carry off the water.

SECTION III.

ON THE TRACE OF WORKS.

11. We must now consider the subject of the *plane*, or *trace*, of works of defence, and the following terms require to be defined:

When the parapets forming an angle contain between them a portion of the space occupied by the work, it is called a *salient angle*—when the contrary, it is called a *re-entering angle*.

The angle contained by the crest of a work (or its prolongation), and that of another work which flanks it, or defends its front, is called the *angle of defence;* and the lines forming that angle are called *lines of defence*. The line bisecting a salient angle is called the *capital*.

12. Before proceeding to describe the outlines used for field-works, the following general rules or principles may be laid down as applicable to all fortifications, whether temporary or permanent:—

I.

13. *The contour of an intrenchment should be proportioned to the number of men intended for its defence.* (See Art. 29.)

II.

14. *The works should be so traced that the ground*

over which an enemy must pass to approach any part of them should be swept both by the direct and flank fire of the defenders.

III.

15. *The flanking parts of a field-work should always be within easy musket range of every part of the lines they flank.* In field fortification, no line of defence should be made more than 180 yards long, until rifles are generally introduced.

IV.

16. *Every part of the works themselves should be flanked by some other part*—that the assailants may be seen by the defenders in every step of their attack.

V.

17. The longer lines should, if possible, be traced so that their prolongations may fall upon marshes, valleys, or water, *in order that it may be difficult to enfilade them.*

VI.

18. The works should be placed so that *they may cover the space enclosed by them against the fire of the assailants.*

VII.

19. *The defence should always be as direct as possible.* The defence is called *direct* when the flanking line is perpendicular to the line flanked; when not perpendicular, it is termed *oblique defence.*

An angle of defence should be a right angle, or a slightly obtuse angle; for as a soldier, when placed behind a parapet, usually fires in a direction nearly perpendicular to that parapet, if the angle of defence were less than a right angle, part of the fire of one parapet would be directed on the crest of the other; which, if it did not occasion accidents, would at best be a mere waste of ammunition. If, on the contrary, the angle of defence were made very obtuse, the salients would be ill-defended, because the fire of the flanks would be directed too wide of them. As it is important to flank the ground just outside of the ditch, an angle of 95° may be considered the best in general.

VIII.

20. *The salient angles of works should be made as large as possible, and never less than* 60°. This rule is to be observed in order to diminish the space QAP, Fig. 3, being that over which the enemy's columns can advance to the attack with-

out receiving the direct fire of the work. If a salient angle were made less than 60°, the interior space also would not be of sufficient width to permit of artillery being placed near the angle, and the parapets would unite in a narrow ridge, not sufficiently substantial to resist either the effects of heavy rains, or the fire of the enemy's artillery.

21. In the following descriptions of the outlines of field works, the lines considered as the outline of construction are the interior crests of the parapets.

SECTION IV.

OF OPEN WORKS.

Of the Redan.

22. A work formed of two *branches* or *faces* uniting in a salient angle (BCA, Fig. 3),* is called a *redan*.

The open or rear part of the redan, and of all other works, is called the *gorge*. It may be perceived that a redan would be of little value unless

* All the figures of general outline are drawn on a scale of 100 yards to an inch; those of detail on a scale of 14 feet to an inch, excepting where it is otherwise specified on the Plate.

the gorge were well defended by other works, or by obstacles to an assault. The redan, therefore, is only used to form part of a line of works intended to cover a camp, the front of a position, or the advanced posts of an army, or the avenues of a village, farm-house, or bridge. The principal defect of this work is that it has an undefended ditch—a defect common to most of the isolated works usually constructed in the field. If at the point A, perpendiculars AP, AQ, to the faces AC, AB, are traced, it will be perceived that the space QAP is deprived of direct defence, and consequently favours the enemy's attack. This defect may be partly remedied by filling up the salient angle as far as MN, thus forming an interior thickening of the parapet without altering its external appearance. The faces of a redan may be of any length; but when the form of the ground permits, they are usually made about 50 yards long.

To increase the strength of a redan, flanks, CE, BE, Fig. 3, may be added. These flanks should be not less than 10 or 12 yards in length, and should be placed within 50 or 60 yards of the salient or *flanked* angle, in order that the attacking column may be exposed to an effective musketry fire from them, before it reaches the counterscarp.

Of the Lunette.

23. The lunette is a larger work than the redan, composed of two faces, AB, AC, Fig. 4, and of two flanks, BD, CE. These flanks are intended to give a direct defence to such portions of the exterior space as could only be seen obliquely by the faces of the lunette.

The lunette is sometimes closed at the gorge by a stoccade, but, like the redan, is frequently open there, and if so should be only applied in the cases mentioned in Art. 22. This work is often used in the field on account of its simplicity, and the facility with which it may be adapted to the ground.

Although a great variety of dimensions may be given to the faces and flanks of a lunette, yet on level ground, it may be traced with those marked in Fig. 4; its trace should however be adapted to the form of the ground, and be such as to defend the approaches as directly as possible, so that its salient will usually be more obtuse. The angles ABD, ACE, are called *angles of the shoulder*.

The defects of the lunette are similar to those of the redan; it has undefended ditches, a large space opposite the salient angle deprived of fire, and two smaller spaces opposite the angles of the shoulders; the last defect may be remedied by cutting or rounding off the angles B and C, and the first partially so, by similar operation.

Of the Double Redan.*

24. A work composed of two redans, connected together so as to defend each other, is called a *double redan*.

This work consists of two faces, AB, CD, and of two flanks, AE, EC, Fig. 5. The double redan being open at the gorge, ought, like the lunette and the redan, to be defended by natural or artificial obstacles, or by works in its rear. It is often used to cover a small bridge, in which case its faces should be defended by batteries placed on the opposite side of the stream or river.

The flanks EC, EA, defend the salient angles B and C; but the ditches, excepting opposite the salients, are no better defended than those of the redan and lunette. When the double redan receives no flank defence from works in its rear, flanks *ef* may be added to the faces, as described in Art. 22. Fig. 5 is the plan of one of which the salient angles A and C are about $75\frac{1}{2}°$.

The angle AEC is a right angle, and it is so made that the two salients may be directly defended by the flanks.

In determining the length of the flanks AE, CE, it is to be observed, that if these lines were made very short, they would of necessity afford only a feeble fire, and also that the men mounted on the banquettes, near the re-entering angles, are pre

---

* *Fr.* Bonnet de Prêtre.

vented by the adjacent parapet from seeing the bottom of the ditch opposite the salient angles A and C, so that their crests must extend at least as far as the prolongations of the counterscarps of the ditches to be flanked by them. The flanks should therefore never be made less than 15 yards, nor much more than 30 yards in length, because the space then occupied by the work would, in most cases, allow of the adoption of a better description of outline.

SECTION V.

OF ENCLOSED WORKS.

25. If an isolated spot is to be occupied and its gorge is unprotected by natural obstacles, or other works, the intrenchment must be continuous, and enclose a space sufficient to contain its garrison.

When the outline of the enclosed work is so traced that the ditches are in general flanked by the parapets, it is called a *fort*; when no part, or only small portions, receive flank defence from its parapets, it is called a *redoubt*.

Of Redoubts.

26. A redoubt may be either circular, quadri-

lateral, or polygonal. The defects of a circular redoubt are, that it is difficult to apply to irregular sites, and that it distributes its fire equally on every part whether required or not. It is more usual, therefore, to give redoubts a quadrilateral or polygonal form; tracing the principal faces to defend directly those parts over which the enemy can most easily approach, and giving either a polygonal, indented, or curved form to the other parts of the redoubt, so as to adapt it in the most advantageous manner to the ground which it is required to occupy. On the side least exposed, or most convenient for communication, an opening EF, Fig. 6, is left; and that the enemy may not, through this opening, see in reverse the defenders of the redoubt, it is covered inside by a mass of earth GH, raised in the form of a parapet, and called a *traverse.** In some

* To determine the length of traverse required to cover a given passage, and to represent the sloping sides of the passage, as seen in a plan. Draw on the same ground-line, MN, Fig. 7, profiles both of the parapet and of the traverse, making the distance apart equal to that intended to be left between the bottom of the exterior slope of the traverse and slope of the banquette. Complete the plan of the parapet and traverse as directed in the note to Art. 6. Make EF equal to the width of the passage, and draw EG, FH, perpendicular to the crest of the parapet. Set off externally, from the lines EG, FH, a fractional proportion of the heights A,B,C, and D, equal to the base of the sloping side of the passage usually ¼, ⅓, or ½, of those several heights. Through the points so found draw E *a b c d* G, and you will have a true representation

cases a work may be advantageously entered from the ditch, through a covered gallery or postern, Fig. 51; a road or ramp being left on the side of the counterscarp, by which to descend from the exterior.

27. Traverses without banquettes are often constructed in works to give protection against the effect of shells and of ricochet fire, and to cover the interior space from the view of the enemy on neighbouring heights. Traverses with banquettes increase the means of active defence also; in large works, the defenders may rally behind them, and fire from them, or rushing *en masse* upon the assailants, before they have formed in sufficient numbers to render further defence unavailing, drive them out, and regain possession of the work.

of one side of the passage, the other being constructed in a similar manner. A man of ordinary stature fires at an elevation of a little less than $4\frac{1}{4}$ feet above the ground: suppose then the profiles of the parapet and traverse to be cut by a horizontal plane at that height. Draw a line, PL, parallel to the ground line, and $4\frac{1}{4}$ feet above it, to represent the trace of that plane. Project on the plan of the parapet and traverse the intersections of the line PL with the interior and exterior slopes of the parapet and exterior slope of the traverse. Through the intersections of those lines with the slopes of the passage previously determined, draw the lines ST, S'T', and make the traverse 4 feet longer at each end than is given by the line TT', to allow for the partial destruction of the sides of the passage and ends of the traverse.

28. The principal defect of square or quadrilateral redoubts is, that they present to the assailant four undefended spaces opposite the angles, so that they may be attacked on four equally favourable points at the same time. This defect may be partly remedied by filling up the salients, as in Fig. 3, making short faces there about 6 yards long.

Some authors recommend an indented parapet to obtain fire from the salient angles of works, as in Fig. 8. These indented parapets are, however, so difficult of execution that they can rarely be applied by the practical engineer; it may also be observed that there is as much fire lost in front of that part of the face occupied by the indented parapet, as is gained on the salients.

29. To determine the proper dimensions for works, so that they may be proportioned to their garrisons, the following points must be considered.

In a square redoubt, the interior slopes and banquettes, if for single rank, occupy a space 11 feet wide, round the interior area; the side of that area, therefore, is 22 feet less than the side of the square formed by the crests: and it is necessary in most cases that an enclosed work should contain a traverse, unless closed by a musket-proof gate, and also that there should be an open space for the accommodation of its garrison: it follows, therefore, that the length of side of a square re-

doubt has an inferior limit, to find which the following data may be assumed:

Suppose that each man requires three feet lineal of parapet, and 15 superficial feet of the interior space—that the traverse to cover the passage into the work occupies 1000 feet of the same space, and that the interior slopes of the opposite parapets, treads, and slopes of the banquettes make the side of the interior space 22 feet less than that of the crest of the parapet; if then the number of men to defend the redoubt be n, its interior surface should be $15n+1000$; and if x be the length of the side of the redoubt in feet, $4x$ will be its perimeter, and $x-22$ the side of the interior space, the area of which will be $(x-22)^2$? To determine x and n we have then the following equations, supposing the work to be defended by a single rank only,

$$\frac{4x}{3} = n \quad \ldots \ldots (1)$$

$$(x-22)^2 - 1000 = 15n \ldots (2)$$

Whence we get $x=71$ feet, and $n=95$ men. The smallest square redoubt should, therefore, have a side of 71 feet, and contain a garrison of 95 men.

If the redoubt be defended by two ranks, each banquette must be made $1\frac{1}{2}$ feet wider, and the solving equations will be

$$\frac{8x}{3} = n \ \ldots \ \ldots \ (1)$$

$$(x-25)^2 - 1000 = 15n \ \ldots \ (2)$$

Whence we obtain $x = 94$ feet, and $n = 251$ men.

When the redoubt is to contain a reserve of one-third of the whole garrison, the second equations will be the same as in the preceding cases; and for the first case the first equation will be

$$\frac{4x}{3} = \frac{2}{4}n \ \ldots \ \ldots \ (1);$$

for the second case,

$$\frac{8x}{3} = \frac{2}{3}n \ \ldots \ \ldots \ (1).$$

When a redoubt is to be thrown up, no time for calculations can generally be spared, and it is not at the moment when one is required to act, that the pencil should be resorted to; but it will then be necessary to recollect the principal results given in the table, art. 31, and not to go below their limits.

To find the greatest or least length for the side of a square redoubt armed with artillery, subtract for each piece 15 feet from the length of each rank broken by it, in the first equation; and from the interior space, in the second equation, 600 superficial feet for each piece, which will allow room for the gunners and ammunition.

30. When a redoubt is defended by a single

rank only, it is evident that every casualty must tend to diminish the quantity of fire from the parapet; no important work should, therefore, be so garrisoned. If defended by three ranks, two of them stand on the banquette; the first rank fires, the second loads, and the third rank supplies casualties, and removes the killed and wounded from the banquettes; but it is much better to have, instead of a third rank, a body of picked troops kept together as a *reserve*, ready to charge the enemy on any point where he may penetrate, before he has time to form. With two ranks the second performs the duties of the second and third; and a work so manned may be considered capable of making a formidable resistance.

To determine the requisite garrison for a work already constructed, a case which will often occur; allow two men per yard lineal of the parapet of the principal faces, and one man per yard lineal of the remainder of the parapet, having previously deducted 15 feet from its length for each piece of artillery.

This will be a sufficient force for works supported by troops, or other works, in their rear; but if unsupported, not fewer than two men per yard of parapet should be allowed throughout.

31. The following table shows the proper length of the sides of square redoubts, under various conditions. In this table fractional values have been purposely omitted.

FIELD FORTIFICATION.

Redoubt.	Description of Redoubt.	Pieces of Artillery.	Side of Square in yards.	Number of Garrison	Redoubt.	Description of Redoubt.	Pieces of Artillery.	Side of Square in yards.	Number of Garrison
To be defended by a single rank.	Without a Reserve.	0	24	95	To be defended by two ranks.	Without a Reserve.	0	32	251
		1	26	98			1	33	251
		2	28	101			2	34	252
		3	30	103			3	36	253
		4	31	103			4	37	253
	With a Reserve of ⅓.	0	27	160		With a Reserve of ⅓.	0	38	452
		1	29	165			1	39	449
		2	31	167			2	40	446
		3	32	168			3	41	443
		4	33	168			4	42	440

This table shews that a square redoubt ought not to have more than 42 yards', or less than 24 yards' side; because, passing these limits there will be either too much, or too little interior space. When the space to be occupied is greater than that required for a square redoubt of 42 yards' side, such an outline should be given to the work as may cause the defects of redoubts to disappear, or at least to be greatly diminished.

32. Although field forts are almost always of an irregular form, yet the manner of tracing them on level ground may be pointed out as a model

to be followed, so far as the figure of the ground to be occupied will permit.

Of Star Forts.

33. Star forts on level ground are usually constructed either on a triangle or on a square; in the first case they have six salient points, in the second eight.

The fort with six salients is traced on an equilateral triangle ABC, Fig. 9, of not less than 50, or more than 100 yards' side: each side is divided into three equal parts, and on the central part an equilateral triangle DEF is described. The reason why the sides of the triangle should not be less than 50 yards long has already been given in the latter part of art. 24; and they should not be more than 100 yards in length, because if it were necessary to occupy a larger space than would be required for a star fort of those dimensions, a better outline might be adopted.

The salient E, Fig. 9, is defended by the fire of the lines AF and CD; the salients C and A receiving at the same time a defence from the faces DE and EF; so that the defect of the spaces in front of the salient angles being undefended is much diminished, though not entirely removed.

The six-pointed star fort is imperfectly flanked; the angle EFA being obtuse, the point E can only be defended by oblique fire, which is difficult to obtain from soldiers in the heat of action. This defect is, however, unavoidable, all the angles of the star fort being already at their minimum (art. 20), and consequently not admitting the adoption of any other trace or outline.

34. The star fort with eight points is constructed on a square (Fig. 10.) of from 50 to 100 yards' side. Each side of the square is divided into three equal parts, and on the middle division an equilateral triangle EFG is described. The salient angles of this fort are obliquely and unequally flanked: but this is not so great a defect as to require for its correction the adoption of more complex constructions, simplicity being one of the requisites to be observed in the tracing of field-works. If the work has sufficient interior space the re-entering angles may be retired so far as to make them only 100°, in order to flank the salients better. When symmetry is desired, star forts may be constructed on a heptagon, or octagon, of which the sides are not less than 30, or more than 70 yards long. The salient angles of the crest of the parapet must then touch the angles of the polygon, and be made each equal to 60°.

The principal advantages of an eight-pointed over a six-pointed star fort are, that with an equal perimeter a greater space is enclosed, and when the salient angles are each made equal to 60° the flank defence is more perfect.

35. A star fort intended to be defended by less than 400 men would not enclose sufficient space, and its flanks would be too short. The defects of star forts are numerous, and more than outweigh the advantages before described: the space enclosed is very small as compared with the extent of the parapet; they present numerous faces to the enfilade fire of the enemy, and several points of attack; in the ditches there are many re-entering angles deprived of fire, called *dead angles*, while the number of angles formed by the parapet increases the difficulties of execution. Polygonal redoubts, where means of defending their ditches, described in articles 114, 115, and 116, can be procured, are therefore decidedly to be preferred to small star forts.

Of Demi-bastioned Forts.

36. When the side of a square, or polygon, to be fortified, is from 70 to 100 yards in length, it may be bisected by a perpendicular EF, as shewn in the construction of Fig. 11, the flank GH being made perpendicular to the line of defence AH. The defects of a fort constructed as in Fig. 11, and which is called a *demi-bastioned fort*, are, that on each face there is one dead angle, and that the flank defence of the face GB of the demi-bastion is very oblique.

Of Bastioned Forts.

37. The bastioned fort can seldom be built in the field, as it is difficult to apply it to uneven sites and requires much time and labour for its construction; it should be thus traced, so as to give it the best proportions, and prevent the interior area being cramped:—

Let AB Fig. 12, be one of the sides of a bastioned fort, the following operations are then to be performed on this and on each of the other sides of the fort. Bisect the side AB by a perpendicular CD, equal ⅛ of AB, if the fort be quadrilateral; ⅐ of AB if a pentagon. Make AE, BF each equal ²⁄₇ of AB, and FH, EG perpendicular to AH and BG; join the points G and H, which completes the trace of a *bastioned front*.

Similar operations being repeated on the other sides, there will be as many salient figures, GEA IK, as there are angles in the polygon. These salient parts of the fort are called *bastions*.

38. If in advance of the bastioned front a work *m n o p q* were placed, flanked by the faces of the bastions, and with ditches opening into that of the fort, this work, intended to cover an entrance made in the centre of the line GH, would be called a *ravelin*.

Ravelins are seldom added to forts in the field, but almost always to fronts of permanent fortifications, where they greatly contribute to the defence.

39. In the plan of the bastioned fort given in Fig. 12, there is no undefended point in front, if the dimensions of the front are not too small, for the height of the parapets will not prevent the men defending the parapet GE from seeing the bottom of the ditch from D to H, and those on FH the part GD of that ditch. These parapets will still better defend the ditches in front of AE and BF; so that in the ditch, as well as externally, there is no part which cannot be seen.

The reason why CD is made less in a square fort, than in a pentagon, is, that if it were made $\frac{1}{7}$ of AB, the angles A and B of the square fort would be less than 60°.

The lines EG and FH make an angle of 95° with BG and AH, to obtain a direct defence for the salients. Supposing the relief of the flanks to be fixed, the proper length of the curtain may thus be found: calculate the distances from each flank at which the lines of fire from their crests, with a depression of $\frac{1}{6}$, will strike a plane 3 feet above the bottom of the ditch; and make the length of the curtain such that each flank will defend the space thus shown to be undefended by the opposite one.

The line AB (Fig. 12), is called the *exterior side of the polygon* or simply *exterior side*.

CD is *the perpendicular*.

AH and BG the *lines of defence*.

AE and BF the *faces*.
EG and FH the *flanks*.
GH the *curtain*.

The angles have also their particular names.

A and B are the *salient or flanked angles*.
E and F the *angles of the shoulder*.
G and H the *angles of the flanks*.

40. It now remains to determine what ought to be the length of the exterior side AB.

This length should not be less than 100, or more than 220 yards, a difference which gives great latitude.

It would appear that since the bastioned trace is better flanked than any other, it should be employed in preference to that of the star or demi-bastioned front; but in the limits within which those fronts can be constructed, viz., with less than 100 yards' exterior side, the bastioned fronts would not contain a sufficient internal space; the ditch towards the middle of the curtain would not be seen by the flanks, on account of the necessary height of the parapet above the bottom of that ditch; the flanks would be so short that the greater part of them would be occupied by the parapet of the curtain; and consequently the advantage of reciprocal defence, obtained by breaking the exterior side into faces, flanks, and a curtain, would in a great measure be destroyed. The minimum thus accounted for is only applicable when the crest of the parapet of the fort is not more than 8 feet above the natural level of the ground. If it were necessary to make the parapet much higher, the exterior side of the fort must be increased, otherwise the bottom of the ditch opposite the centre of the curtain would not be exposed to the fire from the flanks.

The maximum is determined by the range of the musket. It is evident that, as the flank HF ought to defend the salient A, it should be within a moderate range of it, or at a distance of not more than 180 yards. With the superior limit fixed at 220 yards, the line of defence AH is about 175 yards long; a length which it would not be proper to exceed until rifles are in general use, because the enemy advancing on the capital of the bastion should be exposed to the fire of the flanks before he arrives at the counterscarp.

41. Bastioned forts require so much labour for their construction that they ought not to be employed for important posts, where they may serve as depôts and rallying points for a retreating army. Forts of the above description should therefore be constructed in the most solid and durable manner; and every means should be employed to render them of a sufficiently formidable character to oblige the enemy to cannonade them with heavy artillery or howitzers, before he can venture to give the assault.

42. The tracing of the counterscarp in the bastioned front requires some particular details. It is done in two ways, either making it follow the sinuosities of the parapet, as in Fig. 27, or the counterscarps of the two faces are continued in right lines, meeting opposite the centre of the curtain, as in Fig. 28; then all the space between the flanks and curtain is excavated, which being a work of great labour, this method of executing it could rarely be adopted. In Fig. 27, a portion of the ditch of the face near each shoulder is undefended by the musketry of the parapet.

To remedy this defect, the counterscarps of the flanks may be sloped off throughout, or at their front ends only, as shewn in Fig. 29, so as to expose the ditches around the angles of the shoulder to the view of the opposite flanks.

This arrangement is advantageous also because it supplies the earth which would otherwise be wanting at the angles of the flank, where the content of the parapet is much greater than that of the ditch.

It might be feared that these slopes would weaken the work, by facilitating the enemy's descent into the ditch; but in field-works the depth of the ditches is not usually sufficient to prevent the enemy leaping into them, so that whether these slopes exist or not, is of little consequence.

CHAPTER II.

SECTION I.

THE TRACE OR OUTLINE OF FIELD-WORKS CONSIDERED IN COMBINATION WITH EACH OTHER.

43. In the first Chapter, the different independent works used in the field have been treated of; we will now consider them in combination, not noticing their height or relief, but only their horizontal projection or plan.

When several works are so combined that they defend one another, they are called *Lines*, and are distinguished according to their arrangements; either as *Continued Lines*, or *Lines with Intervals*; and according to their object, as *Intrenched Camps, Lines of Contravallation, Lines of Circumvallation,* and *Intrenched Positions*.

Of Continued Lines.

44. Continued lines are often used to enclose the suburbs of a fortress, or to connect two strongly intrenched points; they are principally appli-

cable to situations where it is proposed to act on the defensive only, and where they are of so small extent that the whole line of parapet exposed to attack can be occupied with troops, exclusive of the reserves; as, for instance, to close a pass between scarped mountains, or on the sea-shore, or on the banks of large rivers; so as to rest on natural obstacles, which will prevent their flanks being turned. They are often introduced as portions of an extended line with intervals.

Continued lines were formerly used as siege lines—*i. e.*, to blockade a town; but in late wars they have only being introduced for this purpose, when large portions of the place being covered by marshes or inundations, the occupation of the intervening necks of land with continued lines became a work of comparatively small labour.

45. All very extensive continued lines can make but slight resistance, as compared with the labour necessarily expended on them, for the enemy may menace several points at the same time; whence it evidently follows, that nearly as many troops would be required for the defence, as are employed in the attack, which is opposed to the first principles of fortification. Even if the defenders have a sufficient number of disposable troops, they always act under a disadvantage; they must watch and follow every movement of the enemy, and be prepared to resist all his

attacks, whether real or feigned. In continued lines it has often happened that while the defenders were concentrating their forces to resist a false attack, the enemy has penetrated at another point where he was not expected; and a continued line once entered, is generally irrecoverably lost: the success of the assailants inspiring them with additional ardour, while the defenders too frequently give up a position as lost when a proper exertion of manly resolution would have enabled them to maintain it.

46. It may here be remarked that lines, and indeed fortifications generally, should only be considered as accessories: the troops are always the principal defence—the intrenchments merely offer them the means of using their weapons with the greatest advantage, affording them cover from the enemy's fire, whilst he must, in the attack, be exposed to theirs; hence every obstacle that will detain him under the fire of the intrenchment must tend to ensure his defeat.

47. Though the trace of all lines must of necessity be adapted to the ground occupied by them, yet it is necessary that the student should be acquainted with various modes of tracing lines, and with their advantages and defects; at the same time it should be remarked, that the best flanked lines have a more extended parapet than the others, and consequently require a greater force

to defend them, while the labour of throwing them up is proportionably increased. They may be compared by drawing lines shewing the extent of ground swept by their direct fire; they should allow of a powerful cross fire being directed upon the approaches to the salients, and yet must not be exposed to be enfiladed.

On Redan Lines.

48. The most simple outline for a continued line is the following one, invariably used by the celebrated Vauban: he traced the continued line with redans, placed 260 yards apart, and having 30 yards of demi-gorge, and 44 yards of capital, Fig. 13, but this outline of Vauban's is defective, inasmuch as the angles B and C are only obliquely defended by the fire of the curtain AD, or by that of the neighbouring redans, which being placed at a long musket-range apart, would very ill defend each other.

49. The first modification which presents itself to render Vauban's trace capable of making a better resistance, is to place the redans at 200 yards apart; then the salients will be within musket-range of the lines which flank them, but the faces of the redans will still be badly flanked.

It may here be remarked that as the ditches of field works of this description seldom form a great obstacle to an assault, the power of flanking them completely is not so important as the defence of the space in front.

Of Continued Redan Lines.*

50. A second method of correcting Vauban's line, is to break the curtain BD, Fig. 14, forming a redan BCD, with a very obtuse salient, preserving always between the points A and E the distance of 250 yards. This line, though better in some respects than that of Vauban, is far from being perfect. The three angles, A, C, and E, having an equal external projection, are equally exposed to attack, and this is a great disadvantage.

In one point of view, therefore, Vauban's line would be better than a continued redan line, since it presents fewer points of attack, and the parapet from A to D, Fig. 13, cannot be enfiladed.

The salients are usually the points of attack, because the prolongations of the lines forming salient angles can in general be enfiladed by the enemy's artillery; and if the salient points of a position be properly occupied with works advantageously situated, an enemy cannot advance between them, without exposing himself to flank or reverse fire.

To reduce the number of points of attack in a continued redan line, the salients of the large redans may be placed more in advance; giving

* *Fr.* Lignes à queue d'hironde.

to their faces the directions BC, and DC, Fig. 15, nearly perpendicular to the lines AB and DE; to which lines a more oblique direction should be given than in the former trace. Thus only two points of attack, C, F, are presented within the extent of 260 yards, and these salients would be well defended by the fire of the flanks AB, DE, &c., which should be traced so as, if possible, to make angles of 100° with faces.

Of the Tenaille Line.*

51. The tenaille line differs from the continued redan line, in giving greater saliency, and longer gorges to the redans; and making them all equal in size. The defects remarked in the preceding trace are also observable in this one, the three angles, A, B, and C, Fig. 16, having equal projection, are equally assailable; but in the tenaille line the three points of attack extend over a space of 400 yards, while in the continued redan line they occupy 200 only. Another and a greater defect common to all the outlines yet given, except Vauban's, is, that they present long branches to the enfilade fire of the enemy; who, if he attacked lines traced as already described, might place his guns on the prolongations of the long branches, and by ricochet fire not only destroy the artillery and palisading, but also drive away

* *Fr.* Ligne tenaillée.

the infantry from the parapets; he would then advance in columns on the capitals; if the ditch were deep he would throw in fascines enough to enable him to get over it; and when in it, he would be sheltered from the fire of the parapet. It is because all the faces can be enfiladed with equal facility, that the tenaille line appears to be the worst for an open country.

Of Indented Lines.*

52. The indented line is composed of faces, AB, and flanks BC, nearly perpendicular to one another, Fig. 17. The defects of the indented line are, that all its flanks can be enfiladed, unless directed on parts inaccessible to the enemy, and that their shortness prevents an enemy being seen by them, until he has arrived close to the counterscarp of the long branches.

The indented line may be usefully employed in uniting two principal works, A and B, Fig. 18: placed at too great a distance effectually to defend the whole of the intervening space.

If the faces were all traced in the same direction they could all be enfiladed by the same battery, therefore at the centre C, the trace should be changed, that is, on one-half of the line the flanks should fire from right to left, on the other, the reverse; and a cross-fire of musketry is thus

* *Fr.* Ligne en crémaillère.

obtained on the centre, sufficient to defend it, if the works A and B were placed at too great a distance for that purpose. It may be well to observe, however, that the whole of the space between the works A and B should be within the range of the artillery of those works, and that not fewer than three pieces of ordnance should be placed in each of them to flank the approach to the indented line.

Of Bastioned Lines.

53. When only a small length of continued line is required, the method of tracing it shewn in Fig. 19, has been proposed. But if lines of great extent are to be thrown up, more simple outlines should be adopted. The faces CM, CN are made equal to AG or BH, and the flanks Gg, Mm, are perpendicular to the lines of defence. This outline has in some respects an advantage over the common bastioned trace: for if compared with two fronts traced, as in art. 40, on the lines AC and BC, the bastions will be found to be of greater capacity in this; but the curtains are so short in this trace that their ditches would be quite unflanked, and the flank, Cg is too far from B to aid in defending it.

It is difficult to apply bastioned fronts to the ground, and in whatever manner they may be traced, their fire will cross in front of the curtain, but will leave the approaches to the salients imperfectly defended; and there is seldom time to form their ditches so that they may be flanked in reality. (See art. 42.)

54. The indented line connecting two principal works, and continued redan line, with the modification made thereon, possess the advantage of being assailable only at salients placed at considerable distances apart, and which, being few in number, can be the better guarded when the number of troops is small.

In the construction of the work, these parts may be particularly attended to, and strengthened by every method employed in the field, of which descriptions will be given in other parts of this treatise.

The advantage above noticed is so important, that we may prescribe as a general rule, that *works of great extent should generally present strongly marked salient points.*

55. One of the least objectionable modes of tracing a continued line would be to occupy the principal points with redoubts, or lunettes with palisaded gorges, having lines extending between them, of the same profile as the parallels formed in siege operations, Fig. 152, &c., so that troops may advance out of them in line, if opportunity offers; very little labour is required for their construction, and abatis or other obstacles may be

formed along parts of the space in front of such lines.

Works like A and B, Fig. 18, may advantageously be added to continued lines, in order that their fire may sweep the rear of the latter, in case any part is forced, but if placed at a short distance in their rear, they would be less liable to be taken by the enemy, and used by them to dislodge the defenders from other parts.

56. When lines are of a polygonal form, the salient angles made by the sides of the great polygon are the weak points to which attention should be principally directed. When the angle is obtuse, flanks A and B, Fig. 20, may be traced in the forms of redans; but if the angle be acute, as in Fig. 21, then the form ABC, flanked by E and F, may be given to it.

Instead of forming a tenaille at the acute angle, when the point is one of importance, the angle may be cut off by a bastioned front, as in Fig. 22, and if required, the point O may be occupied either by a lunette or a redan flanked by the works in its rear. The salients A and B of the bastioned front should extend a sufficient distance beyond the prolongations OM and ON, of the faces of the lunette, to defend its ditches; which should therefore be made to terminate towards the ends of the flanks in slopes, directed on the faces of the demi-bastions in their rear.

No fixed dimensions can be given for works of this description; they must vary in proportion to the opening of the angle O and the extent of the ground to be occupied.

SECTION II.

OF LINES WITH INTERVALS.

57. In cases where the defenders are capable of offensive movements, lines composed of detached works placed at such distances as to derive protection from one another, and which, being few in number, can be solidly constructed, form secure posts behind which troops may remain in a menacing posture, ready to rush in masses upon the enemy, whenever a favourable opportunity offers. They oblige him, if he cannot turn the position, either to make his attack on a field of battle judiciously selected, and well prepared for his reception, or to remain inactive.

In such cases, success will generally crown the efforts of that army which is best provided with the means of remaining in repose, but is ever ready to take advantage of any false or retrograde movement of its adversary. As an instance, the Anglo-Portuguese army remained a whole winter in the lines of Lisbon supplied with provisions from that city. The French army, comparatively destitute of supplies, finding the position too formidable to attack, retreated to take up a position where their left flank rested on the Tagus, and their front was covered by marshes and inundations; they were thus enabled to detach large parties to collect provisions and forage, and still have their position so occupied as not to risk much if forced to a general engagement: yet the French eventually were compelled to retire.

These advantages continued lines do not possess, for they are nearly as great an impediment to offensive operations, as they are to those of the attack.

It is, however, sometimes necessary to screen the whole area against an assailant's fire by means of continuous lines, which will also be useful in checking his progress in cases where the defenders cannot advance to attack him as above described.

58. In a line with intervals the redoubts, or enclosed works, may be garrisoned by militia or other inferior troops, who, though comparatively useless in the field, will fight behind a parapet, the approach to which is defended by a ditch and palisade.

The columns of troops may then advance through the intervals, to attack, pursue, or annoy the enemy at pleasure, and thus preserve in the defence all the moral advantages of an attack—advantages resulting from the opinion soldiers entertain of their own superiority, when they assail an enemy, or manœuvre boldly in his presence.

59. The following is commonly proposed as a good method of tracing lines with intervals. Upon a first line, generally forming a portion of a polygon or curve, the salients, A, B, C, (Fig. 23) of lunettes are placed, at from 300 to 600 yards apart according to the nature of the missiles used in their defence: their faces are directed on the points D and E of a line parallel to the first, and 150 yards in rear of it—the points D and E, opposite the centre of the spaces AB and BC, indicate the positions of small redoubts, intended to flank the lunettes and defend their gorges. Without this precaution the former would be of less value, for, being open works, the enemy could easily take them, but being protected by redoubts in the rear, they would be of no use to him, nor could he keep possession of them, unless he at the same time overpowered the redoubts. The artillery should be placed both in the redoubts D and E, and in the lunettes, A, B, and C, for though the enemy may take up the prolongations of the faces of the lunettes, and silence any guns placed there; or force the lunettes, and spike the guns; it is indispensable that they should sweep the ground in front thoroughly.

In determining the armament of field-works, it

must always be borne in mind, that the artillery should occupy the most commanding and secure positions; that for the near defence, the parapet required for a gun would be much more usefully occupied by infantry; and consequently, that the artillery is in general more advantageously employed in flanking the approaches to the collateral works, than in the defence of the work in which it is placed; and that, except in large works, artillery, for the reason above stated, weaken the defence: when, therefore, the redoubts are, either on account of the form of the ground to be occupied, or from any other cause, made of small capacity, the artillery should be placed in the most favourable positions outside of the works, covered by low parapets. If the redoubts, D and E, were armed with artillery, the enemy would direct his fire on them; the parapets of the redoubts should be strengthened accordingly; and in order that the prolongations of their faces may not easily be taken up, they should be directed on the salients A, B, and C, of the lunettes.

60. Although the lunettes are not intended to be constantly armed with artillery, barbettes (art. 86) should be constructed at the salient angles to be occupied as occasion may require by the field batteries.

If the line consisted of two rows of redoubts, so placed as to defend each other, the rear parapets of the advanced redoubts should not be made more than from four to six feet thick, in order that they may be easily destroyed by the guns in the second line of redoubts, when their capture renders such a measure necessary.

Lines with intervals sometimes consist of detached redoubts, or forts, placed at the salient and commanding points of a position, either singly or otherwise, according to the importance and extent of the part to be defended.

When a position is occupied in this manner the works should be sufficiently near each other to prevent the enemy passing between them without exposing himself to the effective fire of the artillery in the redoubts, which should therefore not be more than 800 yards apart.

They should contain powerful garrisons; and be easy of access from the rear, otherwise the enemy might pass them. The spaces between the large works, or clusters of redoubts, would then be occupied by the moveable columns of infantry and cavalry, from which the garrisons of the works would receive reinforcements, ammunition, or other required assistance.

In bold and rocky positions, many portions of a line may, with comparatively little labour, be rendered nearly or wholly inaccessible by scarping the slopes, in doing which, great care must be taken that the base of the parts cut down may not form a road or resting-place, of which the enemy might avail himself.

61. An advantageous and economical mode of tracing a line with intervals, when thrown up in a level country, is to suppress the second line of redoubts, and replace them by one or two large central works, sweeping with their fire the intervals and interiors of the lunettes.

Upon an arc of about 900 yards' radius, and which may be marked by estimation on the ground, the salients A, Fig. 24, of lunettes, are placed 300 yards apart.

In the centre O of the radius AC, a central work should be constructed, such as a polygonal redoubt or star-fort to contain heavy ordnance.

The flanks D of the line must be strongly supported by works, or natural obstacles, that the enemy may not be able to turn the position. The redoubts D on the flanks should have slight parapets or palisades only towards the central work, that they may be easily destroyed by the artillery of the principal work.

At the points of junction of the lines of defence, epaulments, P, cover the field artillery, placed there to flank the faces of the lunettes, A. These epaulments should only be 3 feet high, that the guns may fire over them; their construction would, therefore, be a work of small labour, yet they will be of great assistance. In this arrangement of lines with intervals, the interior of the lunettes is well defended by the central work, on which the principal labour and care should be bestowed, this being the principal point; and it might be built with bastions or kaponiers to flank it.

62. If the position exceed 1,800 yards in extent, it would be necessary to have two or more arcs similar to the one already described, supported in the rear by a bastioned fort, or by polygonal redoubts.

Works of small importance, such as redans for instance, should be thrown up in the re-entering angles, formed by the meeting of the arcs, these points being strong in themselves. It must be evident that the tracing above described for lines with intervals can only be applied to fields of battle prepared at leisure, and that the localities may make it vary infinitely; but it is the spirit of the arrangement, rather than the arrangement itself, which it is in all cases desirable to seize, that we may not err against principles when compelled by local circumstances to depart from regular forms.

CHAPTER III.

SECTION I.

OF THE EXECUTION OF THE WORKS.

Profiling.

63. HAVING given a general description of the plan and profile of such works as are commonly used in the field, the details of construction remain to be pointed out.

When a work is traced on the ground, i. e., after strong pickets have been driven at all the angles, and the lines joining them have been distinctly marked with a pick-axe, two profiles should be set up on each line, to show the workmen the form of the parapet, and to guide them in the execution of their task.

On long faces, three or more profiles should be set up. These profiles, when made with straight slips of deal or other wood, show with great accuracy the form of the parapet, &c. To set up a profile, first drive two square-headed pickets A, B, Fig. 26, marking the width of the parapet; then nail firmly to A an upright slip AC, equal in length to the height of the parapet, and at B set up a piece of indefinite length; nail a slip CD, at C, and with a level * give it the proper slope of the parapet; saw off the over-lengths of BD, and CD, and place DE at an angle of 45°. The banquette is similarly treated, as shown in the Figure.

64. If profiles are set up shewing the several angles formed by the parapet, they will be of great assistance to the workmen.

To put up oblique profiles, first set up two profiles perpendicular to the parapet of each face, then determine the point in which the projections of the exterior crest meet at the angle, which may be done by tracing, with tapes or lines, parallels to the interior crest previously marked on the ground with the pick-axe. At this point set up a slip or pole of indefinite length, and at the angle of the interior crests, one to shew the height of the crest of the parapet; nail a slip of deal to the top of this last upright, and move it up and down on the other until you find it in the same plane with those shewing the superior slopes in the perpendicular profiles; do the same for the exterior slope, and the banquette.

* The field-service level, invented by Lieut.-General Sir C. Pasley, R.E., will enable an officer to determine immediately any slope the base of which is a fractional part of, or equal to, its height, whether the slope be measured from a horizontal or vertical line.

When slips of deal cannot be readily procured, drive in rough stakes to mark the several heights of the profiles, and stretch a piece of cord from one to another to shew the slopes. If the above assisance cannot be procured to regulate the height of the parapet, it rarely would be necessary to model it accurately; the object is to procure cover, and this may be done without the aid of profiles. Having set up the profiles, trace with a pick-axe * the scarp and counterscarp lines.

65. The width of the berm must depend on the nature of the ground on which the work is constructed; in marshy soil it might be necessary to have a berm of 6 feet, or more, while, on the contrary, in a stiff clay no berm would be required.

66. Though the ditch, when of uniform width, supplies a superabundance of earth at the salient, and too small a quantity at the re-entering angles, yet in field-works this is a matter undeserving of notice; yet it may not, however, be unnecessary to remark, that it is better to trace the ditch too narrow than too wide; then, if little time be allowed for its excavation, a ditch of proper depth is obtained, which can at any time be widened, if required.

67. In the field, an officer has not always time to set up profiles before the workmen arrive; in which case he determines quickly the general out-

* Termed "spit-locking."

line of the work by angle pickets; and having marked nearly the position of the middle of the ditch, places the workmen there, directing them to what width and depth they are in the first instance to excavate. In the mean time he sets up profiles, and traces the lines of the scarp and counterscarp as before directed.

Division of Labour.

68. The arrangement of workmen in such a way that they may not incommode each other, and that the work may proceed with regularity, is a very essential matter. The following methods are recommended:—Divide the working party into squads of six men each, one with a pick-axe, one with a shovel and rammer, the remainder each with a shovel: the pick-axe, with a shovel on each side, is placed in the ditch, two shovels on the berm, the shovel and rammer on the parapet; each squad occupying 10 feet lineal, measured on the line of the centre of the ditch. A second method is to divide the ditch into rectangles 3 feet wide, extending in length across the ditch; sixteen men will then be required for every 24 feet lineal of the ditch—eight with a pick-axe and shovel each, four with a shovel and rammer each, and four with shovels only. The first eight excavate the rectangles, as marked in Fig. 30, the odd uumbers

commencing at the berm and the even ones in the middle of the ditch, all working towards the counterscarp; and when the even numbers arrive there, they return and begin at the berm. Four shovellers are placed on the berm, each occupying 6 feet lineal of it, and the remaining 4 shovellers and rammers on the parapet, spreading and ramming the earth. If the parapets were only to be 6 or 9 feet thick, two men on the berm and two on the parapet would be sufficient. A third method, is to divide the ditch into rectangles as before, 6 feet wide each; then place three men in each rectangle, one with a shovel and rammer on the parapet, the second with a pick-axe and shovel excavates from the berm towards the counterscarp, and the third excavates the part of the rectangle next to the counterscarp, heaping the earth on a ridge left for that purpose, between him and the other man working in the same rectangle.

By the first method, 140 men are required for 80 yards lineal of the ditch; by the second, 160 or 140, in proportion to the thickness of the parapet; by the third 120 men.

In addition to the above working party, sappers, or other intelligent men, are employed in forming the revetments, laying platforms, building powder magazines, &c.

69. The ditch is excavated in layers of 3 feet

in depth, steps being left with a rise of 18 inches each, to facilitate the ingress and egress of the workmen, and of such a width that their re-entering angles may coincide with the slopes of the scarp or counterscarp, Fig. 25.

When the ditch is excavated to the required depth, the steps are first cut down with a pick-axe, and the slopes are then dressed with a shovel if neatness of appearance be desired.

Care should be taken to preserve the good earth to form the slopes of the parapet. For this purpose fat earth mixed with strong sand is the best.

When works are hastily thrown up, the vegetable mould, which is generally the best for forming the slopes, is covered by the lower strata; when these latter are, as is often the case, full of small stones, the earth first excavated should be thrown on one side, to be afterwards used as a cover for the parapet. If this precaution were not taken, many casualties might occur from the effect produced by the enemy's shot striking on the stony surface of the parapet.

In selecting the site of a work, rocky situations, but slightly covered with earth, should be avoided.

70. From the commencement of the work attention should be paid to the draining of its interior. When the work is open at the gorge, a small trench may be formed at the lowest part of it, and the terreplein be sloped towards the trench and

gorge. In enclosed works, a covered drain should be constructed to convey the water from the lowest point of the interior into the ditch, taking care to prolong this species of tunnel with planks or other means beyond the base of the scarp, so that the water may not wear away that slope. A couple of planks may be nailed together to form a gutter, which can be let into the slope of the scarp, and the drain be made to empty itself into the gutter, the bottom of which should rest on a few flat stones or ends of fascines. When practicable, the ditches of field works should also be drained, otherwise the scarp and counterscarp slopes will not stand long, unless they are revetted.

71. In all cases, work should be given either by task or at a certain sum per cubic yard of excavation, &c., for men will do much more when tasked than when paid by the day. If peasantry are employed, it is much better and cheaper to pay a high price for measured work, than to employ them by the day.

As soon as the price is fixed you are at ease, for then the work will certainly be done quickly, and you have only to superintend its execution, and see that it is done properly, for task-work will generally be ill done, unless the workmen are well looked after, because it is their interest to finish it quickly.

To fix the price of labour, employ a few good workmen, pay them well, and see how much they can do in a given time; you may then calculate what would be a fair remuneration, and make your bargain accordingly. In favourable soil, an expert workman can excavate from 8 to 10 cubic yards in a day of eight hours' work; but this is only when the excavation is near the surface, and the earth is thrown at once on the parapet. When the excavation becomes deeper, or the earth is gravelly and hard, from 6 to 8 cubic yards is as much as can be expected from each workman; and consequently only 4 or 5 cubic yards per man when a row must be placed on the berm, for an extra line of shovellers must be provided if the earth has to be thrown beyond a distance of 12 feet horizontally or 6 feet vertically. When near the surface, in soil requiring the use of a pick-axe, 6 cubic yards would be a fair task for soldiers who are unaccustomed to the use of the pick-axe and shovel.

72. In calculating the time required to throw up an intrenchment, the following additional data may be assumed :—In light, dry, sandy soil, that can be easily dug without the aid of a pick-axe, a man can, in a day of eight hours, dig and load from 19 to 23 cubic yards of earth on barrows. If a pick-axe be required to assist, two men can do the same quantity of work, but if the whole mass must

be first moved with a pick-axe, three or four men should be allowed.

The worst workman may be expected to excacavate at least 15 cubic feet per hour, and throw it to a distance of 12 feet in soil not requiring pick-axes; in harder soil, men with pick-axes must be added in proportion to the difficulty of loosening it.

A man can also wheel 20 cubic yards of earth per day to a distance of 30 yards on level ground, or 20 yards on a ramp. Twenty cubic yards of earth will fill 500 wheel-barrows. A horse can do as much work as seven men; he can carry 300 lbs. 20 miles per day, or 200 lbs. 30 miles; he can draw 1600 lbs. on a plain, and from 1200 to 1300 lbs. on irregular ground, when the roads are in good order.

SECTION II.

OF REVETMENTS.

Parapet Revetments.

73. It has been stated that a base of one foot only should be given to the interior slope of the parapet. Earth freshly dug up will seldom stand at this slope, it must therefore be supported by a *revetment*, which is commonly made with fascines, hurdles, sods, planks, casks, gabions, or sand-bags.

Fascine Revetments.

74. Fascines are bundles of brushwood bound tightly: those used for a revetment should be strong, and securely bound. When small brushwood is used they are made 6 feet long, and 7 inches in diameter, firmly bound with 4 or 5 withes or gads, one in the middle, one at each end, and one in each interval. The gads are made of tough twigs, first twisted until the fibres separate, the smaller end is then turned round so as to form a loop or noose, as in Fig. 31. To make a fascine 6 feet long, the workmen set up three fascine-horses on the same level, and in a right line. The fascine horse is formed of two pickets, 5 feet long each, driven about 1 foot obliquely into the ground, so as to cross each other at right angles 2 feet above the surface of the earth, as in Fig. 32, and fastened together at their point of meeting with cords or gads. The brushwood, stripped of all its leaves and smaller branches, and which should be from $\frac{1}{2}$ inch to 1 inch in diameter, and 5 or 6 feet long, is then laid on the fascine-horses, the thick ends being placed alternately at each end.

The large stuff must be used to form the exterior, and the smaller twigs the interior of the fascine.

Before binding the fascine, it must be compressed with a fascine choker, which consists of a cord or chain equal in length to $1\frac{1}{2}$ times the circumference of the fascine, fastened at one end to a lever 5 feet long and $2\frac{1}{2}$ inches in diameter, with a loop at the other end, into which, after passing the chain round the fascine near the part to be bound, a lever, similar to the one already described, is inserted, and the brushwood is squeezed tightly together until the gad is tied. The fascine must be compressed in a similar manner before each gad is fastened, and be measured with a cord to ascertain that it is of the required size, unless a mark be placed on the chain of the choker to show when it is of a proper thickness. The weight of a fascine of this kind is about 33 lbs.*

Three men can make a six feet fascine in 20 minutes. Two of the workmen place the brushwood, while the third prepares the gads, which is the only difficult part of the operation, and requires previous instruction.

75. If large brushwood can be procured, the fascines should be made 18 feet long, the strength of the revetment being materially increased by diminishing the number of joints, and using fascines of greater diameter. When the fascines are

---

* This weight must evidently be very variable, depending on the description of wood used, and its degree of humidity.

F

18 feet long, they are made 9 inches in diameter, and the gads are placed at 18 inches apart.

The fascine-horses for these large fascines should be placed one yard apart, in a right line, and on the same level, otherwise the fascine would be crooked and troublesome to work with. A fascine of the above description weighs about 2 cwt.

Four men can make an 18 feet fascine in two hours, or if the wood be cut and brought to them, they can make four fascines in the same time.

They require three bill-hooks, one saw, one fascine choker, (each lever about 6 feet long), and six fascine horses. Three men prepare the brushwood and lay it on the horses, while the fourth makes the gads.

When three or four thread spun-yarn can be procured to tie the fascines, it will save much time and labour.

76. The revetment is formed in proportion as the parapet is raised, the first fascine being one half buried in the banquette, with three pickets driven vertically through it, each picket from 3 to 4 feet long, and from $1\frac{1}{4}$ to $1\frac{1}{2}$ inches in diameter, at the thickest end. The second row of fascines is then laid a little in front of the first, so as to form the required slope, and three pickets are driven through each fascine, the extreme ones through the fascine previously laid in the direction of the slope, the other perpendicular to the slope.

The Austrians, instead of the middle picket, use an anchoring picket driven into the middle of the mass of the parapet, and a long withe or cord, being passed round the centre of the fascine, is secured to the end of the picket, as in Fig. 38, &c.: great stability is thus given to the revetment of the interior slope. The joints of the different rows of fascines should be so broken, that no two adjoining ones may be in the same line, and the ends of the fascines at the angles should alternately be flush with, and be inserted in, the parapet; care being taken to lay the fascines so that the ties of the gads may be concealed in the parapets.

Six rows of large fascines are sufficient to form the revetment of a parapet, the upper row being covered with a layer of sods, the grass upwards. When fascines of 7 inches in diameter are used, eight rows are required.

Hurdle Revetment.

77. The hurdle revetment is made by driving strong pickets 18 inches or 2 feet long into the earth, from 8 to 10 inches apart, in the direction of the slope: flexible branches or rods are then interwoven between the pickets, all the ends being inserted in the parapet.

The upper layer of rods is secured with gads to the pickets, to prevent the work getting undone.

To counteract the thrust of the parapet, each

picket should be secured with two or three anchoring pickets as represented in Fig. 53.

This kind of revetment is easily and speedily formed; and if proper care be taken in its construction, it will be found to be a very good one.

Sod Revetments.

78. The third kind of revetment is made with sods of unequal sizes, called headers and stretchers. The headers are 1 foot 6 inches long, 1 foot wide, and $4\frac{1}{2}$ inches thick, if the soil will allow of their being cut to that depth.

The stretchers are 1 foot wide and long, and $4\frac{1}{2}$ inches thick. Sometimes the sods are cut all of the same dimensions, viz, $1\frac{1}{2}$ feet long and 1 foot wide; the sod is then cut diagonally across so as to form two, and they are then all laid as headers. This saves nearly half the turf and labour. The sods should be cut from meadows well provided with grass previously mown, and if possible, watered, that the earth may more firmly adhere to the roots of the grass; but the sods should not be laid or built when wet, because they would shrink in dry weather, and all the joints would open; if when laid, they are moderately dry, the revetment will always keep solid.

The sod-work is laid with the grass downwards, either alternately as headers and stretchers, or two stretchers to one header; care being taken that the joints of no two rows fall immediately over one another: this is termed *breaking joint*. If the layers of sods are laid perpendicular to the slope, they will resist the thrust of the parapet better than if laid horizontally. Each sod should have two or three pegs driven through it to secure it to the work beneath. The sod-work should be carried up at the same time the parapet is formed and the earth near it be well rammed. If layers of small brushwood can be procured to mix with the earth of the parapet, as represented in Fig. 25, it will contribute to the stability of the work.

When the revetment is completed, the whole should be cut off smooth to the proper slope; a pair of hedge-clippers, or a cutting knife, will answer well for this purpose.

Revetments of sod-work are capable of being made with great perfection, and when so made, are very durable: they are therefore commonly used where nicety of appearance is required. One man can lay 19 square yards of sod-work in a day of eight hours, when the sods are brought to the spot, and require no previous trimming.

79. To cut the sods form the meadows, first trace with a spade or pick-axe lines to mark the dimensions of the sods, or, to trace these lines, a small description of plough, drawn by five or six men, migh be used. As soon as the compartments are marked, the sods are cut with a sharp-pointed

spade made for the purpose, or they may be traced and cut with a common spade.

Revetments of Planks, &c.

80. When neither fascines nor sods can be procured, as will often be the case in besieged towns, the floors of the houses will always afford an abundant supply of materials for forming the revetments of the interior intrenchments, which in their details of execution are similar to field-works.

If plank or timber cannot be procured, a good revetment may be made by mixing the most binding earth which can be found with chopped straw or rushes; this being wetted and well rammed, will form a very solid and durable revetment. The parapet should never be revetted with masonry, except in situations where artillery cannot be brought to attack the work, as the splinters caused by shot striking it are very dangerous. Casks may often be used with advantage to revet the interior of works.

Revetment of Gabions.

81. Gabions are cylindrical baskets open at both ends, and are very commonly used to revet parapets: they are made of various dimensions: for the interior of parapets they should be 3 feet in

height and diameter. The common gabions, viz. those used by sappers, are two feet in diameter, and 2 feet 9 inches high. To make them, a directing circle, consisting of two hoops kept apart by bits of wood, to which both hoops are secured with pack-thread, is first made. The diameter of the hoops must be such as to permit of the pickets for the gabion being driven between the exterior of the one and the interior of the other, as shown in Fig. 147. The directing circle is then laid on a level piece of ground, and seven, eight, or nine pickets are driven at equal distances apart, between the hoops, the number of pickets depending on the size of the rods or brushwood with which the basket-work is to be made. The circle is then raised, and fastened to the middle of the pickets, and the web is made above it, two or three rods being used at the same time, the workman twisting them round each other while he interlaces them with the pickets; striking down the web from time to time with a stick, in order to give the basket-work as much solidity as possible. The *randing* or basket-work is continued nearly to the top of the pickets, where it is secured with four *gads*, each one passed round one of the pickets, and four or five of the rods; which should be from 8 to 10 feet long, and not more than half an inch in diameter. The gabion is then pulled up, the finished end is placed on the ground, and the directing circle being removed, the remainder of the web is finished and secured as before described. In the above manner two men can make a gabion in ¾ of an hour, using about 80 rods for each gabion.

In forming the revetment, the gabions are placed touching each other with a slope of ¼; the first row is surmounted with two rows of fascines side by side, and a second row of gabions rests on them.

If the parapet have a banquette, a row of fascines should be laid—one half of each fascine below the level of the banquette; and a row of gabions resting on these fascines, with a row of fascines above them, completes the revetment.

Revetment of Sand-bags.

82. This description of revetment is the most expeditiously formed, but being also the most perishable, is only used in cases where cover is required to be speedily obtained; as, for instance, when troops are disembarked on an enemy's coast, where fascines and gabions cannot be procured.

The sand-bags should not be more than three-fourths filled, and the top be loosely tied; they are laid alternately as headers and stretchers, care being taken to break the joints, and to ram the earth of the parapet well, flattening each layer of sand-bags with a smart stroke of a shovel.

Sand-bags are usually made of coarse canvass,

and are put up in packages containing 200. When empty, they are 2 feet 8 inches long, and 1 foot 2 inches wide; when filled, they are 2 feet 3 inches long and 9 inches in diameter. To calculate the number required to revet a given surface, allow 24 sand-bags to 10 superficial feet of revetment.

Scarp Revetments and Stoccades.

83. When the earth will not stand at a slope of $\frac{3}{4}$ as is very generally the case, the scarps of important works should, if possible, be revetted, or supported with timber. Trunks of trees form the best timber revetment for scarps. They should be planted vertically, and be firmly connected, touching each other, their ends being sunk 3 or 4 feet into the earth. A plank revetment, sustained by triangular frames, arranged as in Fig. 33, is sometimes used, when time for its formation can be allowed. This revetment may be made more simple by constructing it as in Fig. 34. It must be admitted as a disadvantage of the revetment shown in Fig. 33, that the parapet cannot be formed until the revetment is completed, on account of the excavations required for the introduction of the frames.

84. If the face of the scarp is not covered in this manner, it should have the natural slope of the earth; and trunks of trees may be placed vertically

and close together either along the foot of it or 4 feet in front of it, thus a line of musketry fire is obtained from behind it, since loop-holes are pierced in the timber 3 feet apart, (see Art. 121,) this is called a *stoccade*. The ditch is made deeper in front than in rear of the stoccade, to prevent the enemy closing on the loop-holes; and ready means of communication between the interior of the work and the ditch should be provided.

85. In well-wooded countries, a stoccade constructed of round timbers, about 1 foot in diameter, and from 10 to 13 feet high, may often be advantageously used instead of earthen works. Fig. 35 is the elevation of a stoccade as above described. If there be no ditch in front, a banquette must be thrown up in the interior, and the loop-holes must be pierced at a height of 6 feet from the ground outside, to prevent the enemy making use of them.

CHAPTER IV.

OF THE DETAILS.

SECTION I.

OF BARBETTES, TRAVERSES, ETC.

86. WHEN field-works are armed with artillery, the guns may be either so placed as to fire over the parapet, or openings may be formed in it called *embrasures*, for the guns to fire through. The first arrangement is adopted when the fire of the guns is required to be distributed over the whole of the space in front of the battery—the last when required for definite objects only.

When the platform for the guns is so raised that they can fire over the parapet, the battery thus formed is called a *barbette*. There are two descriptions of barbette batteries: the first, when the guns are mounted on strong frames provided with trucks and called *traversing platforms*, constructed so that the pieces may be fired over a parapet of the ordinary height; the second, when a part of the interior of a work is filled up to a sufficient height to permit of a gun on a travelling carriage, when mounted thereon, being fired over the parapet.

In the latter case, the *terreplein* of the barbette should be within $3\frac{1}{2}$ feet of the crest of the parapet.

A field-piece requires a space of about 15 feet in width, and 20 in length; so that the superior surface or terreplein of a barbette for one piece only would be a rectangle of 15 feet by 20 or 24 feet, the longest side perpendicular to the parapet. (See Fig. 36.)

87. *Ramps* are short roads formed to ascend the barbettes, and for the height commonly required they have a slope of $\frac{1}{6}$, *i. e.*, for each foot in height the ramp should have 6 feet of base. If the height of the ramp be more than 9 feet, the slope must be made less than $\frac{1}{6}$, because it should be proportioned to the duration of the effort required to ascend it. From 9 to 18 feet in height the slope should therefore be $\frac{1}{8}$; from 18 to 27 feet, $\frac{1}{10}$; and from 27 to 36 feet, $\frac{1}{15}$.

Ramps in field-works are made from 8 to 10 feet wide, that there may be sufficient room to drag a field-piece up them.

Sometimes two ramps are formed for one barbette, which facilitates the circulation. In this case they should be placed parallel to the faces of the work, as represented in Fig. 36, which is the plan of a barbette battery for three guns, placed at the salient angle of a work.

Between the guns there are free spaces, the size of which varies in proportion to the opening of the salient angle: these spaces are useful to pile the shot in.

88. We have supposed, in Fig. 36, that a gun requires 18 feet of parapet, in order to obtain room for placing ourselves under cover, which may be done in the following manner :—

To destroy in part the effect of the converging fire, which would be directed against the pieces *en barbette*, if occupying a salient angle, a *bonnette* of earth 3 feet high, is sometimes raised on the parapet between the guns. This bonnette, though it partly protects the guns from the assailants' fire, has the defect of limiting their lateral range, and cannot always therefore be conveniently used. The interior and exterior slopes of the bonnette are continuations of those of the parapet, and a slight superior slope is given to it, to carry off the water. The best method of covering the guns is to throw up a bonnette on their exposed flank only. If the barbette battery cannot be taken in flank by the enemy's artillery, the gunners may be sufficiently covered from the fire of musketry by placing a single row of gabions on the parapet between the guns, with two sand-bags placed on end, one above the other, between each pair of gabions, to prevent the shot passing between them.

89. *Traverses* are high mounds of earth which are very useful in affording protection against the effects of enfilade and vertical fire, and are generally placed across the terrepleins of works.

That the traverse may occupy as small a space as possible, it should be revetted with fascines, or gabions. When made entirely of gabions of a common size, three or four rows are placed touching each other: they are then filled with earth, a layer of fascines is laid on the top of them, and then another tier of gabions, consisting of one row less than at the bottom, a slope towards the interior of the traverse being given to the exterior gabions.

Gabions for traverses are sometimes made from $7\frac{1}{2}$ to 8 feet high, and from 4 to $4\frac{1}{2}$ feet in diameter. Two rows of these gabions make a good traverse.

If intended to resist enfilade fire, traverses should be made 12 feet thick at the top, but if only intended to be *splinter proof*, they need not be more than 6 feet thick. They may often be made useful as *retrenchments* to cut off part of a work, and they should then have banquettes.

One kind of traverse, which has already been noticed in Art. 26, is placed so as to cover the entrance of a work. As these traverses are intended to resist the projectiles of the enemy equally with the parapets, the same profile must be given to them, and their exterior slopes and ends should, when practicable, be revetted, in order that they may not occupy too large a portion of the interior space.

Larger traverses may sometimes be required in order to cover the interior of a work from the view of the neighbouring heights. The particular method of determining the position and height of these traverses will be treated of in the chapter on "Defilade;" passages should be formed in them to communicate between the different parts of the work, and powder magazines may often be constructed in them with great advantage.

Of Passages.

90. Passages through traverses may be made with great gallery frames and sheeting, art. 207, or with fascines only. Figs. 47 and 38 shew the manner of forming these passages.

The fascines for the top should be stronger than common fascines; they are made 12 feet long and 11 inches in diameter.

The passages should be $6\frac{1}{2}$ feet high in the clear, and $6\frac{1}{2}$ feet wide at the bottom, to admit of the passage of artillery.

When formed with gallery frames, the frames should be placed 3 feet apart from centre to centre. The passages must be made at the same time that the traverse is thrown up, and if a great mass of earth be required above the ceiling, they must not be covered with fascines. Then strong timber should be laid across the top, viz., beams 10 inches square, or rafters, flooring joists, or planks on edge with short bearings, covered with boards or fascines. The passages forming the entrances to works are generally uncovered, and cut through the parapet in the least exposed parts; that they may be of as little detriment as possible to the defence, their sides should be revetted at a steep slope, the bottom being made only of sufficient width to permit the passage of artillery, viz., $6\frac{1}{2}$ or 7 feet.

These passages are usually closed either with a barrier, or *chevaux-de-frise*, the manner of constructing which is explained under the head of "Barriers," art. 97, *et. seq.*

Bridges at the Entrances.

91. To communicate with the interior of a work, a bridge must be formed across the ditch. This bridge will generally consist of two parts, one standing or permanent, the other moveable; but if the ditch be not more than 12 feet wide, the whole bridge may be made moveable. Four or five sleepers laid across the ditch, of not less

dimensions than 6 by 4 inches, are covered with plank; a piece of smaller scantling is laid on the top of the plank immediately above the exterior sleepers, to which it is secured by *rack-lashings*, notches being cut in the ends of two adjoining planks for their introduction. The rack-lashing consists of a piece of stout rope fastened to the thick end of a pointed stick, the rope is passed round the pieces of timber to be secured, then twice round itself, as in Fig. 39; the end of the stick is then put into the loose *gromet* so formed, and twisted round until the whole is firmly secured, when the stick is turned flat on the upper piece of scantling.

When the ditch is more than 12 feet wide, a trestle or frame, as represented in Fig 40, must be placed in the middle to support the sleepers. The transom, or upper piece, should be 10 feet long, and the legs should be further apart below than above, in order to give steadiness to the bridge.

When a bridge is more than 24 feet long, two or more such frames must be placed in the ditch to support it. These frames should not be more than 12 feet apart. The sleepers should be from 7 to 8 inches square, and all except the last bay of the bridge may be permanently fastened; a baulk being nailed over the planking on each side of the bridge, to prevent the wheels of carriages, &c., going too near the sides.

92. When rough timber only can be procured and no plank is available, a bridge may be formed much in the same manner as already described: stout straight limbs must be selected for the sleepers which should have but short bearings; they may then be covered with short hurdles, over which a layer of sods, and then a small quantity of gravel may be laid.

Of Powder-Magazines.

93. Magazines are often constructed either in the interior of traverses, or by the side of them.

Sometimes large casemates of timber are formed in the interior of large traverses to serve as magazines and barracks; but this would only be done in works of importance. These magazines and barracks may be formed in the same manner as the passages, with frames and sheeting. Field powder-magazines should not be made to contain so much powder as would cause great damage by its explosion, and the powder required should be divided, and placed in separate magazines (one to 4 pieces of artillery).

94. The best description of field powder-magazine is constructed of splinter-proof timbers about

10 inches by 8, placed against the rear of a substantial and well-revetted traverse at an angle of from 45° to 50°, Fig. 41, and strengthened externally with sod-work 2 feet thick, or earth in sandbags, the whole covered with tarpaulins; or the tarpaulins may be placed next to the splinter-proof timbers, or with an intervening row of sandbags only; it is not then exposed to external injury, but if accidentally damaged, it can be readily repaired. If the site of the work be favourable to drainage, the floor of the magazine may be sunk 2, 3, or even 4 feet below the surface of the earth.

A passage to the magazine may be made with common gallery frames and sheeting, or in the same manner as covered passages, Fig. 38.

Magazines are sometimes made with horizontal roofs, or as in Fig. 42, with a double row of splinter-proof timbers meeting in a ridge; the bottom frame of the magazine should then be strongly connected at both ends, and at intervals of about 6 feet, by stout timbers framed into, or halved and bolted, to the long sides of the rectangle, as in Fig. 43; the ends of the splinter-proof timbers are then notched to fit into the bottom frame or sill.

When timber cannot be procured for making magazines, casks or barrels may be buried in a traverse, in the reverse of a barbette, or in the parapet, to contain a small stock of ammunition.

Of Embrasures.

92. Embrasures are formed in the parapets of field works when the guns are required to fire only in a particular direction, as before explained in art. 86, such as to flank a scarped slope, ditch, abatis, or wall, &c.

In order that the men who serve the guns may be little exposed, the interior opening or *neck*, of the embrasure should not be more than 2 feet wide, and its *cheeks* or sides should be built up with a small slope.

The outer opening of the embrasure measured on its *sill* or *sole*,* under the exterior crest, viz. EF, Fig. 44, is usually made equal to half the thickness of the parapet, and is called its *mouth*. That part of the interior slope of the parapet immediately beneath the embrasure is called the *genouillère*; its height for field-guns should be $3\frac{1}{2}$ feet. If the cheeks of an embrasure were of too great height, the explosions of the gun would soon occasion their fall, and thus render the embrasure unserviceable. For the above reason, the sill of an embrasure should, in ordinary cases, not be more than 4 feet below the crest of the parapet;

* From *Fr.* " seuil," a threshold.

if, therefore, the parapet were more than 7½ feet high, it would be necessary to raise the terreplein and the platform for the gun. The portion of parapet contained between any two embrasures is called a *merlon*.

The most solid revetment for the cheeks of an embrasure is one like that formed with plank and timber, as in Figs. 33 and 34, the only difference in the arrangement being, that the plank should be fixed outside the upright timbers, so as to present a smooth surface for the cheek of the embrasure, instead of being introduced behind the timbers as shewn in those figures. Large fascines, are, however, more generally used for revetting embrasures. The ends of the fascines are laid flush with the interior slope of the parapet.

Under the exterior crest each fascine is made to cover not much more than half of the one next beneath it, being withdrawn towards the interior of the merlon, so that the cheeks of this part form an angle of about 54° with the horizon, and the slope at the neck should be about 6 inches wide at the base for stability. Embrasures are also often revetted with gabions; and in order to protect them from the effects of rapid firing, each gabion is rolled or sewn up in a strip of raw hide.

To trace an oblique embrasure, set off on the directing line CH, Fig. 44, CD, equal to the thickness of the parapet; at D, draw a perpendicular across CD, and make DE, DF, each equal to ¼ of CD: this determines the width of the embrasures at that point; in other respects it is finished as already described.

In Fig. 44 two embrasures for guns are shewn, and also the plan of embrasure for a howitzer, marked A: the sill of this embrasure falls from the exterior crest towards the interior of the work, so as to increase the cover, as howitzers are usually fired with some elevation; and its neck is made 3 feet wide, as the muzzle of a howitzer projects much less than that of a gun, and would injure the cheeks by its explosion, if the width were not increased.

Of Platforms.

96. To facilitate the working of a gun it must be placed on a platform of timber and plank, but when required to fire only in one direction, planks laid for the wheels and trail will suffice.

Platforms behind embrasures should have an inclination of 6 inches towards the parapet, to check the recoil, and facilitate the running up of the pieces, but those on barbettes, or for mortars, should be perfectly level.

When a gun is required only to fire in one direction, the platform should be rectangular, 10 feet by 17 feet for heavy artillery, and 9 by 15 for field guns. Mortar platforms should be 7' 6"

× 6′ 6″. The dimensions for the platforms of barbettes must depend on the extent of lateral range which may be required.

In laying a gun-platform the first thing to be done is to fix the *hurter*, which may be a piece of timber 7 or 8 feet long, and 7 inches square; or a strong fascine may be used. The hurter is intended to receive the wheels or trucks of the carriage when the gun is run out, and to prevent their damaging the interior slope of the parapet. The position of the hurter necessarily depends, therefore, on the steepness of the interior slope, and the size of the gun-carriage wheels. The hurter should be placed perpendicular to the axis or central line of the embrasure.

Five sleepers, from 5 to 8 inches square, are then laid, parallel to the axis, with their upper surface level with the bottom of the hurter, and they are covered with two-inch plank, nailed or racked down in the manner described in art. 21.

Of Barriers.

97. The entrances to enclosed works are generally secured either by *barrier gates*, or *chevaux-de-frise*.

When the passage into a work is only 6½ feet wide, a single gate will be sufficient to close it. This gate should not be less than 6½ feet high. It is usually composed of two upright *stiles*, and two horizontal *rails*,* framed together, and strengthened with a diagonal brace, represented in Fig. 45; six or eight palisades of about four inches square are halved into these pieces, and spiked at all the halvings. Stout hinges are nailed, or fastened with screw-bolts, to the rails.

The gate turns between two posts each about 1 foot square, their ends sunk 3 feet into the earth, and connected by a sill of similar dimensions 1 foot beneath the level of the ground. The gate is hung to one of the posts, and a slip of wood is nailed to the other to take the barrier when closed.

The gate should open internally, and be fastened with a bar of wood or iron extending from post to post.

98. If it were required to close a much-frequented road, the communication by which you wished to preserve, as is always the case when the environs of a town or village are intrenched, the barrier gates should be 10 feet wide in the clear: and should consist of two parts, similar in construction to the barrier already described. In the centre of the sill, a piece of iron or hard wood must be fastened to take the lower ends of the barrier; and braces should be framed into the angles of the sill and posts, to prevent the wheels

---

* The rails are frequently cut out of beams 7″ × 7″. The section of the rail is then a trapezoid, and its parallel sides are 5 and 2 inches long.

of carriages damaging the gate-posts, as well as to strengthen them.

Of Chevaux-de-frise.

99. The chevaux-de-frise, when intended as a barrier, is made of a piece of wood equal in length to the width of the passage, and about 1 foot square, or, if round, 1 foot in diameter, traversed by several pointed poles or spears $6\frac{1}{2}$ feet long, Fig. 46. The spears are commonly placed so as to present two rows of points to the enemy, and they should be of sufficient strength to prevent a man breaking them. One end of the chevaux-de-frise sometimes turns on a pivot, and the other is supported by a wheel, which facilitates its movement; this end is brought against a stout post, to which it is secured with a chain. The spears of the chevaux-de-frise should be so arranged as to present three rows of points to the enemy, as in Fig. 46. Sword-blades are sometimes used instead of these spears.

SECTION II.

OF OBSTACLES.

100. Having given a general description of the

details of the construction of intrenchments, we will proceed to point out some of the means of adding to their ordinary strength, and thus rendering them capable of greater resistance: and it must not be forgotten that their strength depends in a great measure on the *amount and duration of the fire* which can be directed from them upon an enemy advancing to the assault, which is of course increased by *delaying the enemy* when under its influence; whilst the *moral effect* of a check caused by unexpected obstacles is also very great, and time is thus gained, so as to render a surprise more difficult.

The ditches of field-works are in general but a slight impediment to the enemy's progress; for if they were not more than $6\frac{1}{2}$ or 8 feet deep, as is often the case, it would be very easy to leap into them, though incumbered with the weight of the knapsack and musket. Unless a work has flank defences, the enemy when in the ditch, is no longer exposed to the effects of musketry fire, and they could soon cut down, or surmount, the obstacles placed there; it is therefore desirable in such a case to place as many obstacles as possible in front of the counterscarp; bearing in mind always that the more completely these obstacles are under the fire of the works the better they will fulfil their object. But if the front of an obstacle can be flanked when placed in a ditch, it will not only be difficult to cut it down, but it will be thus well protected against the effect of artillery fire.

Of Abatis.

101. One of the best obstacles which can be formed is an abatis, consisting of stout limbs of trees, well twisted together, stripped of leaves and small branches; the large ones being pointed, and turned towards the enemy, presenting to them a great number of points, as in Fig. 47.

These limbs or branches may have their thick ends buried in the earth, or be secured to strong stakes driven into the ground; and be covered from the effects of the enemy's fire by a glacis, the slope of which should be directed to the crest of the parapet in the rear. The earth required to form this advanced glacis may be taken from the rear, by producing the slope of the inner glacis; and in this excavation the abatis is placed. See Fig. 47.

When placed in the manner above described, it does not mask the fire of the work, and cannot be easily destroyed by the enemy.

There is no reason why the advanced glacis may not be of the same height as the inner one, but it is almost always made lower. It would be useless attempting to fix dimensions for works of this description, which vary with every different situation. All that is necessary to observe is that the slopes of the glacis should be seen by the work—the crests should be at least 5 feet below that of the parapet—and the abatis be covered from the direct fire of the enemy. The labour of dragging the trees required, from a distance, is so great that the construction of abatis should not be attempted if none grow near at hand.

Hard and tough woods are the best for an abatis: pine is the worst, for it is easily broken, and burns readily when fresh cut, which is not the case with hard woods. The abatis should not be felled long before it is wanted, that it may not get too dry.

This is of all obstacles the easiest of execution. It is but imperfectly replaced by *chevaux-de-frise*, which are difficult to make, and should therefore be rejected as an obstacle, except on a very small scale.

Of Military Pits.

102 Military pits, or trapholes,* are excavations formed either in the shape of an inverted cone or square pyramid.

They are usually placed in two or three rows as in Fig. 48, outside the counterscarp, and principally opposite to the salient angles.

In the centre of each pit, a pointed palisade or stake is fixed with its point level with the ground.

* *Fr.* Trous de loup.

The pits are also used in situations where cavalry could not approach.

They should be made 7 or 8 feet deep, that the enemy may not use them to fire out of. Even if made only 2 or 2½ feet deep, and well staked at bottom and in the intervening spaces, they will be a good obstacle. The earth excavated from the pits may be formed into a glacis to conceal them, or to cover an abatis in front. In this case, the small branches cut from the abatis may be laid over the pits, that the enemy may not be able to distinguish, and by leaping, avoid them.

Of Inundations.

103. When field-works are constructed near a rivulet, the water should be retained by dams, that it may accumulate in front of the intrenchment, and thus form an inundation; indeed, if the dams can be placed so as to be secure against the enemy's fire, the inundations will afford such security that no parapets will be necessary in rear of them.

If the ditches of a work can be filled with water, it forms an excellent means of defence, and must not be neglected, since it completely remedies the defect of dead angles, and greatly increases the difficulty of carrying the work by assault. This remedy has, however, its inconveniences: in winter, the water may freeze, and then the ditch will be altogether useless. The only means of obviating this disadvantage, is to break the ice every morning and evening, and throw water on the parapets, which when frozen, would render them so slippery that it would be difficult to get over them.

When the inundation is shallow, ditches should be cut chequer-wise through it, of about 12 feet long, 6 feet wide, and of sufficient depth to prevent men wading through them. These cuts will render the access difficult, as their position is concealed. The earth excavated should be spread abroad, that all parts may be covered by the waters of the inundation.

104. If the intrenchments are traversed by a rivulet perpendicular to their general outline, and the waters can be retained by forming a dam of the glacis or parapet of the intrenchment, the inundation will offer a great obstacle to the flank movements of the enemy; and if you have established a ready communication along the rear of your intrenchments, it will enable you, when his attack is decided, to withdraw your troops from that part which is not threatened, and to meet him on either side of the inundation with the whole of your forces.

An inundation parallel to an intrenchment is not, in general, so advantageous as one perpendicular to it; the former having the disadvantage of being as great an obstacle to your attack as to that of the enemy. It may indeed compel him to direct his attack on some other portion of your intrenchments, and thus reduce the assailable ex- extent of the position.

The dams of a parallel inundation are in most situations more easily assailed than those of an inundation perpendicular to the intrenchment, be- cause, in the first case, the dam is perpendicular to the intrenchment, consequently one end is at a greater distance from your works than the other, and the necessity of having those points well de- fended will often lead to so extensive an arrange- ment of works as could not be with propriety undertaken in the field; while the dam, in the latter case, may sometimes be within your line of works, and form one of your communications across the stream.

105. Dams may be formed with a rough frame- work of timber supporting a mass of earth, having a thick coat of clay to prevent the water finding its way through. They should not, in general, be made higher than 12 feet, and must be provided with proper weirs to carry off the surplus water safely. See Art. 175, &c.

Of Pickets, &c.

106. The small branches cut from an abatis may be rendered useful by making pickets of

them; and after driving them into the bottom of the ditch, or between the military pits, cutting the ends exposed to a point, allowing them to project about one or two feet above the ground, as in Fig. 47.

If the ground on which the entrenchment is thrown up be covered with vines or low bushes, the vines should be left intact. The stems of some of the bushes should be cut into pointed pickets, and those of others only half-way through, so that they may be bent down, and the boughs of the brushwood lying across, and being interlaced, they will thus form a very good obstacle, called *an entanglement.*

On the glacis, *harrows* may be buried with the spikes exposed; or broken wheels, and large rough stones, may be strewed about, to break the order of the assailants in a night attack. In warm climates, there are many plants of rapid growth which form powerful natural obstacles; such, for instance, as the aloe. A good aloe, or prickly-pear, hedge is one of the most impenetrable natural obstacles that could be presented to an enemy.

Of Crows' Feet.

107. Crows' feet are formed of three or more short stout spikes, connected together at their larger ends, so that in whatever position they may

be placed, they will always have one point upwards. They are principally used as an impediment against cavalry.

Of Palisades and Fraises.

108. Palisades are made of large branches of trees, or young trees split or sawn into two or more pieces, according to their size. They are often of a triangular form, each side of the triangle being 7 or 8 inches long. Each palisade should be about 10 feet long. To plant it, a narrow trench is dug, from 3 to 4 feet deep, in which the palisades are placed upright, 4 inches apart. The earth is then filled into the trench, and well rammed to secure them below; and they are nailed to a beam or "riband" 4 inches by $2\frac{1}{2}$ inches, either within 1 foot of the top of the palisade, or near the bottom of it. The riband must be placed on the inside of the palisade. It would be an advantage to have them also nailed to a riband concealed in the ground, that the enemy might not be able to pull them up singly.

If the palisade be required to remain long in the ground, the ends should be charred or partly burnt; it will then be less injured by the moisture of the earth.

Oak palisades are the best. The upper part of each palisade is terminated in a point, to which an iron spike is often attached. The best position for palisades is about the centre of the ditch; they are thus sheltered from the direct fire of the enemy, and it may be received as a maxim, that palisades are not of much use if exposed to the enemy's artillery, or unless, while destroying them, he is exposed to the fire of the work. If placed close to the counterscarp, the space between them and the latter may easily be filled up with bags of hay, &c., and they should also be placed far enough back to allow of their front being flanked if possible. Trunks of young trees 14 or 15 feet long have been used as palisades with good effect. If more than 1 foot in diameter, they may be sawn down the middle to form two palisades.

109. Fraises are similar to palisades, but are placed horizontally, or but slightly inclined to the horizon. They are sometimes placed along the top of the scarp, in which case the work should have a glacis to cover the fraises from direct fire; each fraise should be 11 feet long, that they may be buried $4\frac{1}{2}$ feet in the parapet, rest $1\frac{1}{2}$ feet on the berm, and project 5 feet beyond the scarp. The front of the parapet should not be finished till they have been fixed; they are spiked to a riband laid on the berm, and on their upper side another riband is spiked, which being afterwards covered with the earth of the parapet, renders them firm and not easily to be displaced. The points should not be less than 7 feet above the

bottom of the ditch; that men may not easily climb on to them.

110. Fraises might be more advantageously placed 2 or 3 feet below the crest of the counterscarp; there they would be concealed from view, and would not be liable to be damaged by direct fire; the enemy would also be exposed to the musketry fire of the parapet while destroying them. In this case the fraises should be made of such strength as to prevent an enemy breaking them down by his weight, while, to increase the difficulty of leaping into the ditch from the ends of the fraises, the scarp may be carried down to a point, as in Fig. 49.

111. When palisades are planted near the foot of the counterscarp, the ditch may be deepened in their rear, as in Fig. 50. This arrangement is advantageous when the ground will stand at a steep slope, for the height of the scarp is thus much increased with little labour; it also prevents the enemy accumulating in the ditch; and consequently the slopes of the scarp and counterscarp should always be carried down to a point, if the ditches have no flank defence.

SECTION III.

DEFENCE OF THE DITCH.

112. In the detached works constructed in the field, the ditches rarely receive any flank defence from their parapets. The enemy, when there, is exposed only to the vertical fire of the work, viz., the hand-grenades and shells thrown by the defenders.

This defect is so material, that in important works no opportunity of procuring flank defence for the ditches, however small in quantity, should be neglected, and the means of doing so will now be described.

Of Stoccades.

113. If the work were a redan or a lunette, a stoccade or bullet-proof wooden wall, as described in art. 84, may be placed *across* the ditch, at the angle of the shoulder, with loop-holes cut in it for the men to fire through: means of getting into the ditch of the flank must be provided, and the work itself must be so situated that it cannot be assailed by the gorge, to make this defence of any service.

Of Kaponiers.

114. For quadrilateral redoubts a small building,

formed of stoccades, may be placed in the ditch at each of two opposite angles, so as to give a flank fire to all the ditches. This work is covered with beams and earth, is made 6 feet wide, and 6½ feet high in the clear, and is called a *kaponier*: its salient is pointed, that it may afford an enemy no cover.

A gallery is driven under the parapet to communicate between the interior of the work and the kaponier, and an entrance may be formed at the end next to the scarp, closed by a barrier 3 feet wide. The kaponier must not extend to the counterscarp, otherwise it will serve as a bridge for the enemy; and in order that its sides may not be shortened, the width of the ditch must be increased opposite the end of the kaponier; small ditches should also be cut in the main ditch parallel to its sides, to prevent the enemy closing on the loop-holes, if they cannot be made high enough, and, as an additional defence, a flanking fire may be obtained from a loop-holed stoccade at the foot of the scarp. These buildings should be placed at the *obtuse* angles of works, in preference to the acute angles, that their flank fire may be as direct as possible; and they must not be exposed to the enemy's artillery fire, whether directed along the ditches or otherwise. Fig. 51 is the plan of a kaponier, combining all the details above mentioned. In Fig. 52 the section of a kaponier is given, with loop-holes pierced near the bottom of the ditch; and this is in some respects a better arrangement than the one before described, this kaponier being less exposed to suffer from the fire of the enemy's artillery, and less likely to assist him in escalading the work, but being sunk below the level of the bottom of the ditch, it would be liable to be flooded, and if another tier of loop-holes could be provided besides those shown in Fig. 52, the defence would be more efficient. Holes must be formed near the roofs of these works, to carry off the smoke.

115. The small width of common ditches, the great quantity of wood, and the time required to construct kaponiers, occasion their being seldom used; and this means of defence can only be resorted to when abundance of time is allowed, and supplies of wood are near at hand, or easily obtained.

Of Counterscarp Galleries.

116. Loop-holed galleries are sometimes constructed of timber, under the counterscarp of the salient angles of works, from which a reverse fire may be kept up along the ditches (Fig. 53). The entrance to the gallery should be closed by a strong door, and a sufficient force to defend it should at all times be shut up in it, when an attack is possible, as the access to it is difficult.

117. Besides the means already pointed out for the defence of the ditch, every kind of obstacle should be there accumulated, and a supply of large stones be collected in the interior of the work to roll down on the enemy.

SECTION IV.

INTERIOR INTRENCHMENTS.

Defensible Barracks.

118. The most certain mode of giving confidence to the defenders, and consequently increasing the strength of a work, is to secure to them the means of retreat; to offer them a last place of refuge, in which they may obtain terms of capitulation, honourable in proportion to the courage displayed in their previous defence.

These interior intrenchments are only applicable to works of great magnitude, and should be constructed of such a form that no part of the principal work may be concealed from their view, and on which their fire cannot be directed. Their capacity must be proportioned to the number of men they are intended to contain, taking care that space for the defence of the main work is first provided; a condition in many cases not easily to be observed. They are commonly made with two rows of stout timbers placed vertically, touching one another, and pierced with loop-holes; they may have a roof formed of stout beams placed at a distance apart equal to their smallest dimension, on which two rows of fascines being laid, the whole should then be covered with 3 or 4 feet of earth. A defensive barrack of the above description is also sometimes called a *block-house*. To expose the least possible quantity of the woodwork, and thus secure it against fire, it should have a ditch about 6 feet wide, and deep, dug round it, and the earth excavated should be heaped against it, up to the bottoms of the loopholes.

The defensive barrack above described should be 7 feet high in the clear, and 20 feet wide; this width will allow of their being two rows of guard-beds, with room to circulate between them. The beds serve as a banquette to the loop-holes.

The length of the barrack must depend on the size of the work in which it is constructed. It may be made in the form of a cross so as to secure good flank defence. In the interior, a magazine should be made; and provisions may be stored on planks suspended from the ceiling immediately above the foot of the bed. The internal arrangements must, however, depend on the form and nature of the ground, which in one case dictates modes of construction that in another would be useless. It is therefore impossible to assign in an invariable manner the form and dimensions of every class of works required in the field: all that can be done is to offer models to be imitated so far as the nature of the case will permit, but which should on no account be servilely copied.

119. In very extensive works an interior redoubt may be made of earth, in which case a small command over the parapet of the principal intrenchment must be given to that of the interior work; not, as might be imagined, to procure a second tier of fire, but that the enemy may not, when on the parapet of the principal intrenchment be able to discover the interior of the inner work; strickly speaking, it would be necessary to give a command of 6 feet to the latter work, which would then not only have a relief of 14 feet above the level of the ground, and therefore pass the limit laid down in art. 62, but would also with difficulty defend the edge of its counterscarp, and the interior of the principal work; its command should, therefore, in ordinary cases, not exceed 4 feet. In these elevated works, the slopes of the banquette should be converted into steps, that the interior space may be as capacious as possible.

An additional cover may, if required, be easily obtained by placing two rows of sand-bags on the parapet, leaving intervals in the lower row to serve as loop-holes.

120. It often happens that the interior defence consists only of a stoccade with flanks, forming an enclosure, a banquette being formed with the earth excavated from a small ditch in front, so that the defenders may be placed above the assailants, and that the latter may thus be prevented from making use of the loop-holes.

These small keeps, though weak in themselves, are of use when nothing better can be built. In the event of a work being surprised, they may enable the garrison to recover from their first panic.

The thickness of stoccades, if made of pine timber to resist musketry fire, should be 12 inches, but if of oak, only 4 inches; to resist field-artillery two rows of timber, each 12 inches square, are required; the second row rising only to the level of the bottoms of the loop-holes.

121. Loop-holes are generally made wider on the inside than on the outside, in order that they may afford as small a mark as possible for the enemy, and yet afford sufficient range for the defenders. The common dimensions are, in walls from 2 to $2\frac{1}{2}$ feet thick,

Interior width.	16 inches
Exterior do.	3
Interior height	18
Exterior do.	33

In stoccades from 6 to 8 inches thick,

Interior width	8 inches
Exterior do.	3
Interior height	18
Exterior do.	22

but the dimensions must be varied according to the object and direction of the fire to be maintained from them.

The height of the loop-holes above the level at which the defenders stand, should be 4 feet; and they should be 6 feet at least above the ground outside in ordinary cases, and about 3 feet apart.

CHAPTER V.

SECTION I.

ON THE MANNER OF FORTIFYING IRREGULAR SITES.

122. WORKS are seldom constructed on level ground, without any irregularities within the range of artillery: they are often placed on elevated spots, but sometimes so near to other heights that if the enemy were in possession of the latter, he could, from them, see the troops in the interior if the parapets were only 8 feet high. This defect can often be remedied by increasing the relief, constructing traverses to cover the interior from the view of an enemy, or excavating the terrepleins.

To adapt the trace to the form of the ground, so as not to require too great a relief, obtaining at the same time cover from the view of the neighbouring heights, and to expose the interior as little as possible to the enemy's fire, without compromising the immediate object of the work, are the most delicate operations required of the field engineer, who must in such cases give up the idea of regularity in the outlines.

Their trace should therefore generally follow the form of the brow of the hill on which they are placed, and their crests should be placed so that they may be in the prolongation of the slope of the hill in front, and that their fire may sweep it throughout.

123. The forms of the heights on which the intrenchments are thrown up, and of those by which they are surrounded, contribute to modify the trace and relief of the works. We shall first treat of the influence of the former, and then point out the means of avoiding the dangerous effects of the latter.

1st. The slopes of the heights on which field-works are to be constructed may be so steep as to be nearly inaccessible.

2ndly. They may be accessible, and yet so steep that they cannot be defended by the direct fire of artillery.

3rdly. They may be gentle, in the form of a glacis.

124. When the heights are nearly inaccessible, works of slight relief should be constructed on the most salient points, and instead of forming a ditch, the slopes may be scarped, as represented in Figs. 54 and 55, and flanked by artillery placed at the re-entering angles of the brow. The notches in

Fig. 54, cut in the original slope, are intended to prevent the newly-raised earth from slipping. The parapets of works situated as above described, unless commanded by the ground in front, would not require to be more than 4 or $4\frac{1}{2}$ feet high; their crests should be brought as near as possible to the brow of the hills; and when not liable to be cannonaded, dry stone walls may be substituted for earthen parapets. In this case a line of works may sometimes be constructed with advantage 200 or 300 yards in rear of those placed along the brow of the hill, so as to receive an enemy, tired with the exertion of mounting it, with a heavy fire.

Small works similar to redans, and called *flèches*, should also be constructed (if the ground admit thereof) in front of, and immediately under the fire of the principal works, both to sweep with musketry fire those parts of the ground which are concealed from the view of the latter, and to afford cover for guns, placed here to flank the approaches to the collateral works, these will often consist of a mere breastwork for the guns to fire over, protected by a high epaùlment on the flank next to the enemy.

The earth excavated to form a terreplein for the guns will supply that required for the parapets of the flèche, which will thus have no ditch in front.

125. In the second case, if the heights present

no salient angles, the works to contain the artillery should be placed in such situations as will enable it most effectually to defend the approaches to the foot of the hill; for as a piece of ordnance, mounted on a common carriage, cannot be fired with a greater depression than $10°$, the ascent of the hill itself could not, in this case be defended by the direct fire of the artillery.

On the crest of the hill, works for musketry should be thrown up, being constructed so that the troops may deploy and attack the enemy in flank, if he mount the hill between those works. The defenders could then act with all the spirit of assailants, and would have the advantage of contending with troops already partly exhausted by their previous exertion.

126. In the third case, which is the most frequent, the works should have a good profile, and be so disposed as to obtain cross fires on all the ground over which the enemy must pass, especially on the roads bridges, and fords in front, and in this case, the works should occupy the crests of the hills.

When the crests of the hills are of no great width, the communications between the several works should be made on the reverse slopes of the heights, where they will be perfectly screened from the view of the enemy. In parts exposed to his view, cover may be obtained by excavating a trench similar to the first parallel made in a siege, Fig. 152, or existing hedges and fences may be strengthened, taking care to secure their flanks.

If, in rear of the position, other more elevated points are occupied with works, the front line of redoubts or other works should be traced in such a manner as to expose their interior to the view of the works in the second line.

When the ground is defended by detached works, they must be either sufficiently near each other to prevent the enemy passing between them, or must be capacious, and contain powerful garrisons; otherwise he would proceed at once to assail the second line, and thus render the first comparatively useless.

When the works in the first line are commanded by the ground *in front* of them, and the ridges of the hills are narrow, the salient faces should be placed so as just to command the approaches, and the rest of the works be laid out on the reverse slopes of the heights.

Works so traced will be much more easily covered from the enemy's fire than if traced in any other manner.

127. If it were required to occupy two heights within range of each other, and to close the valley between them, a redoubt of a good profile should be placed on each of the heights, and they should be connected by an indented line gradually re-

ceding as it descends towards the bottom of the valley. The prolongations of the faces of the indented lines should be thrown on the redoubts, or pass in rear of them; and as they could only be obliquely battered by artillery, the parapets might be made proportionally slight. The flanks would, from their direction, be necessarily exposed to enfilade fire, but being short, this would not cause any great inconvenience. If instead of thus adapting the outline of the intrenchment to the form of the ground, the valley were closed by a parapet traversing it in a right line from one redoubt to the other, either the interior would be exposed to the view of the enemy, or a parapet of great height must be thrown up.

128. It may be required to construct works on the middle of a slope ascending or descending towards the enemy. In this case the most level parts which the different undulations of the ground may present should be carefully sought for, in order to place the parapet on them: however slight the different inclinations of the slope may be, the advantage of this selection will be sufficiently apparent when the work is commenced. If the enemy is expected to approach from the bottom of the slope, the interior of the work should occupy the platform; if from above, this platform should form the glacis, and the interior should be on the slope.

These two arrangements, shewn in Fig. 56, are advantageous, inasmuch as a parapet of small relief will afford good cover to the interior of the intrenchment. In the first case, the superior slope may be made as much as $\frac{1}{4}$; and in the second, it may take, according to the slope of the hill, a contrary inclination, and be directed towards the interior of the work; this is necessary to resist the plunging fire, which would otherwise soon beat down the crest of the parapet.

128. It has been found by experience, that an extraordinary degree of security is given to the artillery in open action, when placed in rear of a brow or slope. Shot striking short have thus as little effect against it as those which are too much elevated, since they ricochet over it.

Parapets for musketry may be constructed on the slopes at any favourable points, as described in the last article, but the artillery should occupy the crests of the hills; and if their height be great, it may only be necessary to level a terreplein for the guns, which would be sufficiently covered by the brow of the hill, when they recoiled, after the discharge, on the surface prepared for them. The artillery so situated may not be able to see the foot of the hills, but its plunging fire would greatly annoy the attacking columns while yet at a distance. Care must be taken to ensure the *drainage* of all works, especially if their terrepleins are excavated.

130. Sometimes it may be necessary to construct parapets on slopes so steep that no ditch can be excavated in front. The earth for the parapet must then be taken from the front or rear as in Fig. 57. These parapets without ditches would be of little value unless they received a good flank defence of musketry, or were protected by some natural impediment. If the materials can be procured, an abatis may be added, laying the branches on the slope, previous to the formation of the parapet with which it would afterwards be covered, Fig. 57.

N.B. The construction of works on the banks of rivers is described in Chap. IV.

SECTION II.

ON DEFILADE.

131. The surrounding heights do not less contribute to modify the outline and relief of works than the irregularities of the ground on which they are thrown up.

The object of *defilade* is so to regulate the relief of the parapets or covering masses, that the defenders may be perfectly screened by them from the view of the enemy.

The direction of a shot is supposed to be a

right line drawn through the axis of the piece, and the point aimed at; for though projectiles move in curves, yet if a point be not seen, it cannot be hit at a short range, with a full charge.

132. If on a horizontal site, the parapet of a work require a command of 8 feet, it must be evident, that, on an irregular site, if the crests of the parapets were placed in a plane parallel to the line ABC, Fig. 58, and 8 feet above it, the interior of the work would be as well covered from *the point of command* C, in this latter case, as in the former. The line ABC represents the *plane of site* as seen in a vertical section, and the corresponding parallel line DEF the *plane of defilade*.

133. When works are placed within range of heights by which they are commanded, the choice of the outline should be principally attended to; for, among the different tracings which may be used, some will be much more easily defiladed than others, and every effort should be made to place them so as to defilade them without giving the parapets greater height than ordinary.

When a work is thrown up opposite to a height, it is the more difficult to defilade in proportion to its depth; it should, therefore, have an oblong form, and in its longest faces should be traced parallel to the height. If, for instance, the work were a rectangular redoubt, the long faces should be traced parallel to the height, and the short ones be directed on it. In selecting the site of a work as above described, if it be defended by works in the rear or cannot be taken in reverse by the enemy, those slopes should be sought for, which, if produced, would pass above, or be a tangent to the ground in front, as in Fig. 58, and on them the interior of the works should be established.

134. It may be laid down as a general rule, that the prolongations of the principal faces of a work should be directed on valleys, or on parts where the enemy cannot place his artillery, within a distance of 800 yards of the salient angles of the work.

It would often be impossible to direct all the faces of a work so as entirely to cover their defenders from the fire from neighbouring heights; some of them will generally be exposed to reverse fire.

Works open at the gorge, such as lunettes, are most easily defiladed: in others, it is often necessary to construct traverses to screen the rear lines from the view of the enemy. When the covering masses are intended to protect the defenders from reverse fire, they are called *parados*. When works require to be supported from the rear, or are used to cover bridges, roads, or dams, &c., they ought to screen as much as possible of the ground in their rear, or of the bridges, &c., they are intended to protect.

On the Practical Methods of Defilading Field-Works.

135. The first operations of defilade are, to determine the extent of the exterior space from which it is necessary to be covered, and the height of the plane of defilade above the plane of site.

In permanent fortification, the horizontal limits extend to 1500 yards from the most salient works, the vertical limit or height being 8 feet.

In field fortification, the limits are regulated by the range of field-artillery and musketry, and by the height at which these arms are usually fired above the ground; for the former, the horizontal limit is 1000 yards; for the latter, 500 yards: and the plane of defilade should be $4\frac{1}{2}$ feet above the ground within those limits, in each case.

136. To give proper cover to the interior of a field-work, the plane of defilade AC, Fig. 59, should pass $4\frac{1}{2}$ feet above the point H, and 8 feet above every part of its terreplein.

The plane DH, Figs. 59 and 61, parallel to the plane of defilade, and tangent to the point of command H, may be called the tangent plane, and should intersect the vertical line AB in the point D, about $3\frac{1}{2}$ feet above the level of the interior: and the plane of site should be $3\frac{1}{2}$ feet below it, and parallel to it, being thus 8 feet below the plane of defilade.

It is required then first to find practically a plane which shall contain the point D, and be tangent to the point H. The following method of finding the required plane is general, and is applied in this example to a lunette.

137. After having planted poles at all the angles of the lunette, Fig. 60, and stretched a cord mn $3\frac{1}{2}$ feet above the ground at the gorge line, hold a straight bar ab between two pickets a few yards in rear of the work; elevate and depress the bar until the lines mn and ab are both in a plane tangent to the height H; if then the eye of the observer be placed at any point of the line ab, the visual ray EH, lying in the plane and cutting the pole at the salient angles of the lunette, will show the height of the tangent plane at the point C. In a similar manner the point D, at the angle of the shoulder, or any other point required, may be found. Saw off the poles at points $4\frac{1}{2}$ feet above these points: their summits will then shew the heights of the parapets required, which should generally be less than 12 feet.

138. In order to reduce the relief, if it exceed the maximum allowed, the line mn may be lowered $1\frac{1}{2}$ feet, which will still leave cover to the height of $6\frac{1}{2}$ feet at the gorge. If this be insufficient, recourse must be had to traverses, or the ground must be lowered at the gorge, which in some cases might be the least laborious operation.

Two or more planes of defilade are sometimes adopted, the interior space being divided into portions, some of which may be covered by traverses, and some by the parapets.

139. With the aid of a plane-table, the tangent plane might be more accurately determined. If the upper surface of the plane-table were placed in a plane tangent to the points of command, the intersections of that surface prolonged, with the pole planted at the angles, would show accurately the heights above the plane of site.

140. If it were required to be defiladed from two or more heights, then the tangent plane being at once tangent to *two* points of the surrounding ground, could not be made to contain on it a given line at the gorge as in art. 137, but only *a point* in it; for instance, a point near the centre of it, which point must be $3\frac{1}{2}$ feet above the ground.

Let H and N, Fig. 62, be two heights from which it is necessary to be defiladed. In the centre of the gorge of the work, or at the point most distant from the given heights, plant a stake projecting $3\frac{1}{2}$ feet above the ground. In front, place two other stakes, D and E, and cause a straight bar to be moved up and down on them, until, when seen from the top of the first stake, it appears to touch at the same time both the points H and N. The plane thus found will evidently be the tangent plane; and to the heights obtained by it, 4½ feet are to be added, as before, to find the heights of the crests of the parapets.

Instead of a straight bar AB, a tape or cord may be made use of, which must be kept stretched tight by persons at each end, who slide it up and down the stakes D and E, until it appears to be in the tangent plane.

141. It often happens, in the case above described, that a single plane of defilade would give too great a relief; the left part of the work must then be defiladed from the height H, and the right part from the height N.

But this arrangement exposes the faces to be seen in reverse, and will consequently render it necessary to erect a *traverse* to cover them; its height should be sufficient to screen the troops, when mounted on the banquette, from the view of the enemy.

The thickness of the traverse at the top should not be less than 8 feet, if intended to resist artillery. Its slopes, unless revetted, are left at 45°.

142. A triangle with sides about one yard long, constructed of smooth laths, having the ends halved into each other, so that the upper and under surfaces may be parallel, is sometimes used to find the tangent planes.

If a line at the gorge, as *mn*, Fig. 60, be given, place one side of the triangle on this line, and move the apex until the surface of the triangle is tangent to the commanding point.

If a point near the gorge be given, Fig. 62, place one of the angles of the triangle on the given point, and move the triangle about that point, until its surface is tangent to the points of command.

143. An enclosed work constructed on the slope of a hill, having a plain on one side, usually requires a traverse to cover it from the reverse fire from the plain; so that a plain is as dangerous to a work constructed on the slope of a hill near it, as the hill would be to a work constructed on the plain.

The most simple mode of determining the form of a traverse is to assume its position, and then give it a sufficient height to cover the men placed on the banquettes on each side of it. At the same time, the planes of defilade of the parapets should pass 8, or $6\frac{1}{2}$ feet at least, above the ground next to the traverse.

144. Let AB, Fig. 63, be the central line of a traverse, and CD, EF, the two opposite parapets of a redoubt, to be defiladed from musketry. On the side of the plain, the parapet EF may be made 8 feet high; but the height of the parapet, CD, on the other side, must be so regulated that the plane of defilade may pass 8 feet above the ground at the side of the traverse.

Draw the lines of fire P*c*, M*e*, which should pass 2 feet above the parapets DC and EF, in order that the shot may be intercepted by the traverse, or pass over the heads of the troops mounted on the banquettes. The height of the traverse is then determined by that line of fire which gives the greatest relief, viz. P*c*, in this case.

For the line P*c*, plant at the point L a pole $4\frac{1}{2}$ feet high; measure on the pole DC, shewing the crest of the parapet, C*c* equal to 2 feet; the visual ray passing through the points P and *c* will be the line of fire sought, and AB will be the height of the traverse.

The other line of fire may also be determined in a similar manner.

Having thus found the relief of the traverse required to cover the widest part of the work, and its command over the parapets being known for that part, let the same be preserved throughout.

These constructions, though simple, require some time: when no opportunity offers of determining accurately the dimensions of the traverse, required to defilade a work, make it one yard higher than the plane containing the crests of the parapet, and the work will, in most cases, be perfectly covered.

145. In a quadrangular work, the traverse should usually be made on one or other of the diagonals, and also be parallel to the height, when

the redoubt is constructed in front of one, and presents one of its angles to the height. See arts. 30 and 31, Appendix.

Defilade of Lines.

146. In the defilading of lines, as in that of isolated works, the object proposed is, to cover the interior space from the view of the neighbouring heights. To obtain this result the same means also are employed, viz. increased relief of parapets, excavation of terrepleins, and construction of traverses, parados, or bonnettes.

In addition to what has been stated in former articles, it may here be observed, that the space within which the defenders are covered by the works should be the greatest possible, the defence of lines requiring large bodies of troops, formed either in lines or in columns.

The choice of a position to be fortified, as well as the particular method of occupying it, by continued lines, or lines with intervals, is, therefore, a matter of very great importance. If any of the heights commanding a position cannot be occupied, epaulments may be thrown up 50 or 60 yards in rear of the lines, to cover the troops intended for their defence. Ramps may be made in rear of these epaulments, for the artillery and cavalry to pass over them; or openings must be left in the most convenient parts for that purpose. The epaulment may have the form represented by Fig. 153.

It is in general not possible to place all the crests of continued lines in the same plane of defilade; they should then be divided into parts, separated by traverses, each part having its own planes of site and defilade.

In note 1 of the Appendix, the problems of Descriptive Geometry which are required to be understood by those who study this subject scientifically, will be found, as well as their application to the most simple forms of field works; serving as an introduction to the more elaborate courses used in military colleges.

CHAPTER VI.

DEFENCE OF RIVERS AND WATER-COURSES.

SECTION I.

OF BRIDGE-HEADS,* AND OBSERVATIONS ON THE BANKS OF RIVERS.

147. RIVERS and streams play a part of consequence in attack and defence; they are, in ordinary circumstances, equally favourable to both armies—affording to both equal security.

This reciprocity will cease if one army, after having established bridges over a river, throw up works to prevent them on the enemy's side. Then an opportunity is afforded of penetrating his country at pleasure, to carry on any offensive operations that may be required, while the bridges secure the retreat of the assailant in the event of a reverse. Everything in this case favours the attack, so long as a communication with the works thrown up to cover the bridges is kept open.

These works are called *bridge-heads:* their

* *Fr.* Têtes de pont.

general arrangement, and particular form, will vary according to the nature of the ground to be occupied, the shape and width of the river, &c.

148. The ground in front of the bridge ought, if possible, to be so occupied as to cover the bridge from the fire of the enemy's artillery; the possibility of this being done depends altogether on the selection of site, in the choice of which many equally important objects require to be considered. The business of the engineer is to cover the bridge, as far as practicable, with few works, requiring small garrisons, that as great a number of troops as possible may be spared for the operations in the field, by which the fate of a campaign is in most cases decided.

From these considerations it would appear that a bridge-head, to cover an important communication, might be advantageously traced in the following manner :—At distances of about 250 yards apart, and 300 yards from the bridge, the salient angles of detached bastions may be placed: these bastions should be closed with a ditch and parapet at the gorge, forming a system of redoubts mutually defending each other. The head of the bridge should be protected by a good stoccade or redan.

The redoubts completed, ditches may be excavated between them, and the earth thrown up be formed into curtains, traverses, and parapets to flank the ditches of the redoubts.

In this manner a defensive arrangement of works may be made, possessing all the advantages of a system of bastioned lines, and requiring only to have three or four redoubts well manned.

Another mode of tracing a bridge-head would be to place lunettes, mutually flanking each other, from 300 to 900 yards from the head of the bridge —their intervals and gorges being swept by the fire of a fort, constructed to cover the head of the bridge, and to afford a place of retreat for the defenders of the advanced works, if the enemy should succeed in forcing them.

By a good disposition of advanced works, the enemy's artillery must be kept at such a distance that no apprehension need be entertained of his being able to destroy the bridges. If the bridge-head be constructed at the re-entering angle of a river, the lunettes or detached works may be traced on a right line, or nearly so, which will both augment the value of the near defence, and diminish the development. In this case, also, the central work or fort may very easily receive a flank defence from batteries placed on the opposite bank, or on the islands which are frequently found at the bends of rivers. The flanks, also, of the advanced line of works would receive a similar defence.

These considerations are sufficient to point out that the best situation for a work to defend the head of a bridge is at the re-entering angle of a river.

149. Instead of being parallel to the frontier, the river may be perpendicular to it, in which case both banks must be occupied by the defenders, and a double bridge-head be constructed, which offers the great advantage of enabling you to oppose the enemy on either bank.

To derive the greatest benefit from a river under these circumstances, several bridges should be established on it; so that if the enemy succeed in cutting off the communication by any one of them, a retreat may still be open by another.

150. The detached works of a bridge-head should be constructed to contain about 200 men each, should have their gorges defended by good stoccades, and in their interior a small tambour or block-house of timber. The salients of these works may be placed 300 or 400 yards apart; for if they have a good relief, and are, as they ought to be, well fraised or palisaded, they will not require such close support as those of the common line with intervals, described in art. 61. It is generally better that the roads leading to the bridges should be constructed round the flanks of the works instead of *through* them.

Lunettes so constructed, with obstacles sufficiently multiplied about them, will, if well defended, render abortive any attempt of the enemy

K

to carry them by assault, without having previously cannonaded them.

If the advanced works were incapable of making an independent defence, their garrison would soon be driven from them; it is therefore desirable to give to those works every possible degree of strength.

151. The intrenchment covering the bridge, being the most important work, must have the greatest care bestowed on its construction. It may be composed of one or more bastioned fronts, having the wings flanked by batteries placed on the opposite bank. The entrances should be on the wings, about 20 yards wide, and covered by interior traverses. An interior intrenchment of wood-work should be constructed immediately in front of each bridge, more effectually to secure the bridges against the enemy's enterprises; who, even if he did succeed in forcing the principal work, might, with the aid of these last intrenchments, still be driven back, or at least be prevented getting possession of the bridges.

One or two batteries should always be placed to destroy the bridges in the event of the enemy unexpectedly forcing the central work and its interior intrenchments or stoccades.

In Fig. 84, a bridge-head is represented combining the several details above given.

152. It will sometimes happen that only one

bridge is to be covered. In this case the central work may be much less extensive, and be composed of a single bastioned front with long branches on its two sides, called a *hornwork*, or consist only of a large double redan, or lunette, defended from the opposite bank, Fig. 85.

These latter arrangements are frequently made when the small width of the stream, and nature of the ground, permit the head of the bridge, and the works covering it, to be well defended from the opposite bank. As to the dimensions of such works, nothing fixed can be laid down; they must vary with every new situation, and the total space enclosed should depend upon the number of troops likely to retreat by the bridges.

Security of the Banks of Rivers.

153. The possession of the bridges is as favourable to the defence as to the attack. Whatever, therefore, may be the attitude of an army, all the bridges in its possession should be covered by intrenchments; but it is also necessary, when acting on the defensive, to watch the fords, and be in a situation to dispute the passage of a river, wherever it presents a favourable point for that purpose.

In front of fords, the general outline of the works should be concave, and batteries should be erected, to rake and flank each ford. The principle on which the works are to be traced is, that the enemy should be exposed to an enfilade fire where the ford is straight, and also to a converging fire, when forming or deploying, after passing the stream. If the space enclosed by the works be favourable to the movements of cavalry, intervals should be left to facilitate their egress from the intrenchments. If the river be wide, and the ford narrow, a redoubt, or lunette, or a battery may be sufficient to defend the passage. A battery* consists of a parapet pierced with embrasures, with epaulments on the flanks, and traverses in proportion to the extent of the battery, to cover the guns from enfilade fire.

154. The salients of a river, corresponding to the re-entering angles formed on the enemy's side, being for the reasons stated in art. 148, the most favourable points for him to establish his bridges, works should be thrown up for their defence, the form of which will depend on that of the ground, the width of the river, and nature of the heights, which may happen to be within range of artillery.

A good redoubt will commonly be the best work to oppose the efforts an enemy may make to establish his bridges. Sometimes, to occupy all the space, one or more bastioned fronts may be

---

* The artillery accompanying an army in the field are divided into batteries, also called field batteries.

required; and in advance of each, a lunette may be placed, the better to discover the banks.

In order to give as great a saliency as possible to these lunettes, they may be thus traced:—After constructing the bastioned front, Fig. 86, join the centres of its faces A and B by a right line, and on this line as a base describe an equilateral triangle A B C; the apex C of the triangle will be the salient angle of the lunette, and the lines CB, CA, shew the direction of the faces, which may be made equal in length to those of the bastioned front.

The ditches of the faces of the lunette should terminate towards the flanks in gentle slopes, directed on the crest of the parapet of the demi-bastions in the rear, in order that they may by seen into and defended by the faces of those demi-bastions.

155. The water-courses separating armies are not always rivers or great streams: they are often rivulets of such small width as to permit of works constructed on one bank defending the approaches to the other.

Such streams should be observed throughout the whole extent of the position, and be defended by detached works placed in the most favourable situations to flank each other, and at the same time to give a cross fire on the fordable points— for the better defence of which, a close and direct fire of musketry should likewise be obtained. A rivulet in this case would perform the part of a wet ditch enclosing the position, if dams were formed across it.

156. When, on account of the commanding heights, the works cannot be placed sufficiently near the banks of the river to defend it well, posts of observation should be established as near those banks as possible; and if the ground be low or marshy, or a portion of the stream can be diverted through it from a higher level, the space in front of the works should be intersected with small ditches, which should be full of water, otherwise they might afford cover to the enemy's rifle-men.

SECTION II.

OF INUNDATIONS AND DAMS.

157. It does not always happen that an army acting on the defensive can find rivers or streams to cover it; but they may derive advantage from the smaller rivulets the country affords, by retaining its waters to form inundations.

As it rarely happens that the means provided for the execution of field-works are sufficient to allow of a dam being made more than 10 feet high; the difference of level between any two dams would in that case be 5 feet, in order that the shallowest parts of the inundation may not be fordable. Having determined the position of the first dam, that of the others may be found by levelling instruments, or from the information collected from the millers of the neighbourhood, with respect to the fall of the stream.

The axis or central line of the upper surface of the second dam should be placed 5 feet below the first, the axis of the third 5 feet below that of the second, &c.; so that the distances of the several dams from one another must be determined by the slope of the ground. It follows, then that this kind of defence is rarely applicable to mountainous countries; it is also inapplicable in extended valleys, unless the banks of the stream are high, and within a moderate distance of each other; otherwise the dams required to retain the waters would be too extensive, and be difficult to defend. No limit can be assigned for the greatest length which may be given to a dam. In one case a dam of 100 yards in length would be a gigantic undertaking, while in another the construction of such a dam would be a work of trifling consideration, as compared with the advantages to be obtained.

158. The profile of dams, and of their waste weirs, does not depend on their length, but on the depth of water to be retained, and their exposure

to cannonade. The details of construction most commonly adopted are as follows.

If the dam cannot be battered by artillery, it should be made 5 feet thick at the top when formed of earth. The earth for the dam should be taken from the valley just below it, in order to give a greater depth to the inundations at those parts.

The lower side may sometimes be constructed of timber, roughly framed together, and covered with a layer of clay, which should be extended into the banks, to prevent the water finding its way round the ends.

If the earth in the immediate vicinity of the dam will not bind sufficiently to prevent the filtration of the water, proper materials must be obtained in the neighbourhood and imbedded in the dam. The best method of preventing filtration is to construct the interior of the dam with well-tempered clay called puddling. In some cases the alluvial soil in valleys will be found to be of great depth; it then becomes very difficult to dam up the waters. If the soil be of a sandy nature, it is not fitted to retain an inundation. When sites of the above description are met with, the bed of the valley or ravine should be thoroughly examined, and the construction of a dam should not be undertaken, unless ample means of execution be provided to ensure success.

When the dam is to resist artillery, it must be made at least 10 feet thick at the top. The exterior slope of the dam may be left at the natural slope of the earth, while, to the interior one, a base of not less than double its height should be given, that it may more effectually resist the pressure of the waters of the inundation.

159. If, after constructing a dam of earth, as above described, the water were suffered to accumulate, and flow freely over every part, it would soon be destroyed, however small the velocity of the stream.

To prevent this, one portion of the dam is left lower than the remainder, and of a sufficient width to give a free passage to all the waters of the stream, or a cut is made round one end of the dam for that purpose.

The surface of the part over which the water is permitted to flow is formed in a more solid manner than the rest of the dam, and is called the *waste-weir*.

The waste-weir is constructed with fascine-work, Fig. 87, or with timber and plank.

After having raised the dam to a height of 1 foot 6 inches less than that required for the upper surface of the waste-weir, a double revetment of well-picketed fascines is commenced, which revetment should not only cover the top of the weir, a portion of its interior, and all its exterior slope, but extend also along the bed of the lower inundation or stream, that the rush of water over the weir may not form pits over the bottom of the dam.

The horizontal fascine-work below the dam should be let into the earth, and be made wider than the rest of the weir. To give greater solidity to the fascine-work, the pickets should be permitted to project above it, and stout twigs be interwoven among them, so as to form a species of hurdlework above the fascines. A much greater number of pickets must be used for work of this description than for common fascine-work, and these pickets should not be less than 5 feet long. The cheeks of the weir, or lateral parts of its opening, may also be revetted with fascines, laid across those forming the bottom of the weir, and firmly picketed to them. There should be four rows of these fascines, so as to extend beyond the ends of the lower fascine-work about 3 feet.

160. To construct the dam, begin by forming the two extremities, leaving the middle open to give a free passage to the waters until the remainder of the dam and the waste-weir are completed. Then fill up the bed of the stream, taking care to connect the new earth well with the parts first executed, and complete the dam.

161. When works are covered by inundations, it may happen that it is desirable to secure the means of letting off the waters at pleasure. This

may be done by means of sluices constructed of wood-work.

The sluice may be made with gates, or consist of pieces of well trimmed timber, grooved and tongued into each other; two stout pieces of scantling being secured to each side of the sluice, to take their ends. This latter arrangement can only be used where the stream is small.

Having a sluice constructed in a dam does not do away with the necessity of a waste-weir, unless the body of water be so small that it may be allowed to flow freely over the gate, or the dam be constructed entirely of wood-work, in which case the sluice-gate may be made to form a part of its opening at the bottom, in a matter similar to the openings made in the gates of locks; the water will then find a passage under the wood-work forming the superior surface of the dam.

Whether gates or sliding timbers are used, the sides and bottom of the sluice for temporary purposes should always be made of wood. Fig. 88, shows the plan and elevation of a sluice-gate worked by two levers. The pieces of timber, laid across the sluice-gate for supporting the levers, may serve to form a small bridge, when it is wished to make a passage along the dam.

162. The waters of an inundation require more or less time to rise to the level of the waste-weir,

in proportion to the velocity of the stream, its vertical section, and the capacity of the inundation.

The engineer should, therefore, ascertain these points, in order not to be deceived in his expectations, and to know what length of time will be required to form the inundation.

To calculate the produce of a stream running in a uniform manner, multiply the mean velocity of the stream by the area of the traverse section of the water formed in its passage through the opening.

The experiments of Dubuat shew, that to determine the mean velocity of a current, when we know the velocity of a surface, V being this velocity in inches, and V' the medium velocity sought;

$$V' = \frac{V + (\sqrt{V}-1)^2}{2}$$

in which expression $(\sqrt{V}-1)^2$ is the velocity at the bottom of the current.

If, then, S be the area of the section of the water-course, T the time sought, and C the capacity of the inundation, we shall have

$$V'TS = C$$
$$\text{Whence } T = \frac{C}{V'S}$$

T will be the time in seconds; C, S, and V must be measured with the same unit, the foot for instance.

163. The end of the dam on the enemy's side must be protected by intrenchments, to prevent destroying it, or using it as a bridge.

When no work can be placed, as will sometimes happen, immediately covering the head of the dam, the approaches to it should be defended; or if the opposite bank be within a short musket-range, the end of the dam may be covered by an abatis. Small islets are often formed in the midst of the inundations, on which batteries and parapets for musketry may be advantageously thrown up, either to protect the dams, or for the general defence of the position. When plenty of heavy timber can be procured, a raft-bridge may be made to communicate with these detached works; or an embankment may be thrown up for that purpose, 10 feet wide at the top: this might, in many cases, be a work of great labour, but it rarely happens that inundations can be formed of very great width, and it is then only that it becomes necessary to occupy the islets. The works thrown up to cover the head of a dam, should be traced on precisely the same principles as those for the protection of a bridge.

The best position for a dam, therefore, when a matter of choice, would be where the opposite bank of the inundation formed a re-entering angle.

CHAPTER VII.

PASSAGE OF RIVERS.

164. The passage of a river in the face of an enemy is one of the most important operations that an army can be called on to execute.

It may be performed either by open force or by stratagem. In the first case, the enemy is driven as far as possible from the opposite shore, by a brisk cannonade, and troops are then pushed over in boats or on rafts, in sufficient force to keep him in check during the construction of the bridge.

165. In the second case, superior forces are to be assembled on one or more points of the river —carriages and boats are to be collected—batteries thrown up, and, in short, every possible demonstration is to be made, to persuade the enemy that a passage will be attempted at one of those points.

When he has concentrated his forces to oppose the anticipated attack, the pontoons, or boats, may be removed during the night to a distance of some leagues, and be ready for throwing over the bridge at the dawn of day. Field artillery accompany the pontoon train, and take post on the banks of the river, so as to give a cross-fire on the ground in front of the intended bridge. Large bodies of troops are immediately passed over, to occupy every favourable point of the opposite bank, and drive off the enemy.

Extra pontoons or boats, should be provided, to be continually employed in the transport of troops to aid those first pushed over, who take possession of any houses, gardens, or other points capable of being artificially strengthened, close up all front and lateral openings, break open communications with their rear, loop-hole the walls, and, in short, do all they can to strengthen their post.

As soon as the bridge is completed, the engineers proceed to trace the works intended for its defence. At the same time that the troops are engaged in effecting the passage of a river, one or more feigned attempts should be made at other favourable points; and be persevered in, with the semblance of obstinacy, if it appear that the enemy has been deceived as to the real intentions of the assailant. The main body of his forces may thus be retained at a distance from the point of passage, until a sufficient number of troops have passed the river to ensure success.* It may be confidently relied on, that an army provided with a good pontoon train cannot be prevented

* See Relation du Passage de la Limat, par Dedon. Paris, 1801.

effecting the passage of a river, if that army be skilfully commanded.

166. The choice of the point at which to pass a river, is a subject involving many important considerations, often at variance with one another.

The re-entering angles formed by the windings of a river are those most favourable to the assailants, not only because the bridges once constructed will there be more easily covered by the works thrown up to protect them, but also because the batteries which support their construction will give a more effective cross-fire on the enemy's shore.

In the great elbows of rivers the current is less rapid than in other parts; and small islands are frequently found there, which facilitate the construction of the bridges, as well as their defence when completed. Choose that part of a river near which bays or inlets are formed, or where another stream emptying itself into it, presents a situation in which you may launch your pontoons, or boats, out of view of the enemy, and whence you may proceed with the current to the intended point of passage. One very influential point in the selection for the passage of a river will frequently be the nature of the roads, by which the pontoon train is to travel to get to the given point, or to some spot at no great distance from which the pontoons, &c., may be carried by working parties to the bank of the river.

Observe whether the opposite bank is easy of access, whether lower or higher than on your own side, capable of being defended by batteries on your bank or the contrary; whether intersected with woods, copses, hedges, walls, or ditches, or otherwise affording cover, which may enable the troops first passed over to keep the enemy at bay, whilst the extra pontoons, boats, and rafts, transport others to their assistance.

Ascertain, if practicable, whether the anchorage be good; for if it be not, great difficulty will often be found in establishing the bridge in a secure manner.

Of Military Bridges.

167. Any description of bridge that can be speedily constructed, and for the materials of which the means of transport can be provided, may be properly termed military. In general a military bridge consists of supporting bodies, *i.e.*, either pontoons,* boats, casks, or floating masses of timber, placed parallel to the banks of the river, at a greater or less distance from one another, in proportion to their strength or buoyancy, and the weight they are required to sustain.

* Pontoons are of various forms; the old descriptions were flat-bottomed open boats; the new ones proposed to supersede them are decked canoes of copper, cylindrical wooden buoys, and tin cylinders; the advantage of which is that they cannot be swamped.

These floating bodies, serving the purpose of piers, in permanent bridges, are connected by pieces of timber called *balks*, which being covered with planks called *chesses*, form the superstructure or floor of the bridge. The space between two supporting bodies, together with that occupied by one of these bodies, is called a *bay*.

The weight a bridge may be required to sustain is the first point to be considered.

Infantry, in two ranks, occupy a space of 3 feet in depth: we may therefore assume that in passing a bridge, formed four deep,* not more than eighty men will be supported on 40 feet lineal of the bridge. Supposing each man with his arms to weigh 200 lbs. on the average, then 16,000 lbs. is the weight to be supported by that length of bridge. If cavalry pass in file, 40 feet of the bridge will have to support eight horses and eight men; suppose each horse and man together to weigh 1400 lbs., than 11,200 lbs. would be the weight of cavalry† on 40 feet lineal of the bridge.

A 12-pounder gun, carriage and limber, weighs

---

* Infantry should never be allowed to pass a bridge formed more than two deep, except the bridge be a very short one; neither should they be permitted to keep step while crossing a floating bridge.

† Cavalry should never cross a floating bridge mounted, if it can be avoided; and all the artillery horses. except the wheelers, should be detached from the guns.

about 45 cwt.: the bearing points of the wheels of the gun and limber are 9 feet apart; the whole gun, together with the horses, occupying a space of about 40 feet in length; but the weight of a

12-pounder, carriage, and limber, is	5040 lbs.
6 horses . .	6048
3 men . . .	450
Total	11,538 lbs.

40 feet lineal of the bridge will, therefore, have to sustain,—with

Infantry, four deep, . .	16,000 lbs.
Cavalry in file . . .	11,200
Artillery (12-pounders) .	11,538

A bridge calculated to support infantry four deep, may, therefore, be passed by cavalry in file, and by field artillery.

The difference of weight between the 12 pounder, &c., and infantry, is required as an allowance for the unequal distribution of the weight of the former on the bridge.

The number of supporting bodies necessary to form a bridge, of any given length, will depend, 1st, on the buoyancy of the body itself; and 2ndly, on the scantling of the timber which can be procured for balks.

When boats are the supporting bodies, take the mean length, breadth, and depth, above the waterline, subtract from the last dimensions 6 inches or a foot, or such other dimensions as the gunwale may be required to remain above the water, when the bridge is loaded with its greatest weight, which dimension will depend on the rapidity and magnitude of the stream.

Multiply together the mean length, breadth, and corrected depth; then each cubic foot of the product will support a weight of 62 lbs.;* from the buoyancy, thus found, must be subtracted the weight of the superstructure required to be borne by each boat; the remainder will be the available buoyancy of the bridge.

If the boats are small they may be connected together in pairs. When large boats only can be procured, and but few of them, bridges may be formed with cables stretched across the river, and supported by these large boats or vessels, in the manner described in the second volume of Jones's "Journals of the Sieges in Spain," p. 104.

The disadvantage of a bridge of this latter description is, that it cannot be partially dismantled, to permit the passage of any floating bodies, sent down the stream by the enemy, to destroy the bridge. Booms, must therefore, be stretched across the river to arrest the progress of those masses.

168. Carts or waggons may often be used as

---

* The specific gravity of the water to be displaced being 1000 ounces per cubic foot.

supporting bodies for a bridge over a canal, or river of small depth.

Each pair of wheels and their axle may have a trestle attached, on which to lay the floor of the bridge.

Timber carriages are well adapted for the formation of a bridge, where the depth of water is nearly uniform, and not very great, as for instance, over canals.

169. A flying bridge consists of a large boat or raft composed of two boats, anchored with a long cable, and which is carried from one bank to the other by the current, according to the direction in which the latter acts upon it.

170. Raft bridges are easy of construction, since they consist only in securing together stout pieces of pine, or other light wood, and covering them with planks or boards; but rafts thus made are not capable of bearing great weights; they are not, therefore, fit for the passage of artillery.

Small bodies of cavalry may be passed over bridges of this kind; the men dismount, and lead their horses in single file, keeping at a moderate distance apart.

The buoyancy of a raft may be increased by lashing empty casks to its side or under it. With the aid of a small pump, a cask may be easily introduced under a raft, by first filling it with water, and then, having secured it in its berth, pumping out the water through the bung-hole.

171. Cask bridges are made by lashing together a sufficient number of casks to form a pier for the bridge which is then divided into bays. The number of casks requisite for each pier will depend on their size, and the buoyancy required to be given to the bridge. Casks may generally be procured in the neighbouring farm-houses, or villages, the floor and roofs of which will furnish materials for your bridge, if no better can be procured.

172. Trestle bridges can only be used for the passage of rivers of small depth, and the bed of which is not very uneven. The trestle may be similar to those described in art. 91, an additional leg being added to the end placed down the stream, to enable it the better to resist the current; this leg is armed with an iron point, the upper end being secured with a hook, to a ring, passing over the end of the transom. The trestles should be 10 feet long; five joists or balks are laid across each bay, their scantling being about 7 by 5 inches; the joists are covered with plank, and side-rails are secured with rack lashings to the extreme balks, as described in art. 91. The trestles should be placed about 10 feet from centre to centre.

173. Pontoon Bridges.—For a description of

pontoons, and the method of forming bridges with them, as well as of the details of raft and boat bridges, and the mode of repairing bridges, &c. &c., the work of Sir Howard Douglas on Military Bridges, and the Aide Memoire to the Military Sciences should be consulted.

CHAPTER VIII.

ON MILITARY POSTS, AND WORKS THROWN UP ON THE EVE OF BATTLE.

174. WHEN villages, hamlets, farms, or enclosures of any kind, are occupied by soldiers, and placed in a state of defence, they are called *military posts*.

The advantage which may be derived from an intrenched village on a field of battle is too apparent to need comment: a post of this kind, when properly defended, will oblige an enemy either to make great sacrifices to get possession of it, or altogether to forego the offensive operations he may have contemplated.

Many instances have occurred where a few brave men, having obtained possession of a farmhouse, or old castle, have defended themselves for a length of time against greatly superior forces. Every officer in the army should therefore be sufficiently instructed in fortification to be able to place a country-house, farm, or village, in a state of defence.

Sometimes a military post forms part of an extensive line, and is supported in the rear by the troops it covers; at other times it is placed in an independent situation, and is left to its own resources.

The post should, in the latter case, contain magazines of provisions and powder, because it may be required to defend it during a long period. In every case temporary cover for the troops, and an interior intrenchment, are essential.

Villages commanded by the neighbouring ground, within musket range, whose houses are much scattered, and which have numerous and wide spaces for ingress, can seldom be occupied with advantage.

Villages built of wood are ill-adapted for defence, for they can be easily set on fire: those built of stone, having the houses grouped together, and the gardens surrounded with walls or strong hedges, are the best for military posts.

175. When an officer is detached to occupy a village, his first care should be to push forward his guards and advanced posts, proceeding immediately to barricade all the entrances on the side of the enemy, excepting only a few small and concealed places of egress. He should next break up the roads by which the enemy can approach the

post: have loop-holes made in all the walls of the gardens, or houses, which his force may enable him to occupy; demolish, or burn detached houses, which would afford the enemy shelter, or mask the defender's fire; and fell all trees which, when felled, would obstruct the attack, or which, if left standing, would impede the defence. The *artillery* should be placed so as to defend those parts most favourable to the advance of the enemy, especially with a view to enfilading the roads, and flanking the approaches; and the pieces must be covered by parapets if possible, and secured against an assault by means of abatis or other obstacles.

If intrenching tools are wanted, the officer will put in requisition every thing of the kind the village or neighbourhood can provide.

While the soldiers, or peasants placed in requisition, are occupied with their first labours, officers are employed to make a detailed reconnoissance of the neighbourhood; others prepare a general plan of the works proposed to be thrown up, which, when approved of, should be immediately put in execution; reliefs of workmen should be provided, and not a minute should be lost, either of the day or night, until the system of defence is completed.

176. If the enemy were to force the exterior intrenchments, this first success should neither en-

sure to him the possession of the post, nor relieve him from the necessity of fighting under a disadvantage. An interior intrenchment should therefore be formed; it will generally be the church and cemetery, or the strongest house in the village, if in an isolated situation, and placed so as to see along the principal streets. This intrenchment should present an exterior defensive line, and an interior point of security, or keep.

Easy communications must be established between the interior and exterior works. If in the immediate vicinity of the village there be any place which may be advantageously occupied, a secure communication should be made between it and the village, either by forming a trench or palisading, unless the detached post be at too great a distance from the village to receive an effective support from it, in which case it would necessarily become an independent point of defence.

Sometimes the village may not contain any building capable of being converted into an interior intrenchment; then the most favourable position in the neighbourhood should be occupied, with works of such a profile as may ensure their being capable of making a good defence, after the village has fallen into the enemy's power.

177. In tracing the defences of the village, advantage should be taken of the walls, hedges,

and ditches, where they can be useful to the defence.

All walls and hedges within musket range, behind which the enemy might conceal himself, should be destroyed, and all ditches parallel to the works be filled up, unless they are wet ones; observing always not to destroy any walls or hedges, &c., which will impede the enemy's flank movements, or check him under fire. In the interior, on the contrary, those walls which obstruct the lateral movements should be broken through, in order to open free communications, and for the same purpose bridges must be thrown over the ditches.

The hedges and walls which will serve to connect the principal intrenchments should be preserved; sometimes they form the only defences, and then care should be taken to preserve those which flank each other.

If the village be traversed by a stream, advantage may be taken of it, to form an inundation; if the stream extend round part of the village, its waters may be retained by a dam, protected by a small intrenchment, or the arches of a bridge may be closed up, so as to make it act as a dam.

Thus, at a small cost of labour, some portions of the village, or other post, may be rendered secure against surprise, and greater forces can consequently be developed on the more assailable points.

Sometimes portions of the ground occupied may be defended by an abatis, having the butt ends loaded with heavy timber, heaped up to form a parapet. The abatis intrenchment offers, in a well-wooded country, one of the most simple and ready means of impeding the progress of an adversary.

178. If the houses are thatched, the thatch should be taken off, because the enemy would otherwise easily set fire to them; and although by so doing he might not succeed in driving out the defenders, it would certainly contribute greatly to their embarrassment. Banquettes may be constructed with planks, doors, window-shutters, or other materials, on the upper rows of beams, or joists, of unroofed houses, whence good marksmen might pour a destructive fire on the attacking troops.

179. The following means are employed to render *hedges* and *walls* serviceable to the defence:—If the hedge be more than $6\frac{1}{2}$ feet high, cut off the branches to that height, and weave in the parts so cut, to strengthen the remainder of the hedge: excavate a ditch in front, without being particular as to its dimensions or regularity of form, and let the earth be thrown over the hedge, and laid against it, so as to form a kind of parapet, of from 15 to 18 inches thick at the top; and with

a portion of the earth a banquette may be made, to enable the defenders to fire over the parapet.

Sometimes you may not have time to make the arrangement above described; then dig a trench in the rear of the hedge, and form the parapet with the excavated earth.

If the hedge were planted on a steep slope, the earth should, as in the preceding case, be taken from the rear.

If the hedge is not $6\frac{1}{2}$ feet high, a small ditch should be made in front, the earth be thrown over the hedge, and a trench be dug in the rear to obtain cover behind the parapet. Or a trench may be dug in the rear of the hedge. two feet deep, and 3 feet wide at the top, and the earth be thrown against the hedge to form a parapet 2 feet high, behind which cover may be obtained by stooping. This trench might easily be excavated in half an hour, and would be of great assistance to light infantry. The hedge thus prepared should not be clipped, in order that the men behind it may be concealed from the view of the enemy, and that it may offer a greater resistance to the assailants when endeavouring to force it.

Fig. 89 represents the five different arrangements above described.

A strong hedge thus prepared is an excellent means of defence. A thin hedge is but a very slight obstacles, and should therefore be avoided.

Neither should those hedges be occupied which can easily be enfiladed by the enemy's artillery.

180. A wall 4 feet high may, without any preparation, serve as a parapet; but if it be 6 feet or more, loop-holes should be pierced. These loop-holes, when they can be of a regular form, as in mud or tapia* walls, are made as described in art. 123 and placed 3 feet from centre to centre.

Loop-holes generally are of an irregular form, pierced in the walls with pickaxes, crowbars, or hammers, and it rarely happens that there is sufficient time to make them in any other manner. They should then be made as small as possible.

To prevent the enemy closing on the loop-holes, a small ditch should be dug on the outside 2 or 3 feet deep, and the earth be laid against the wall. The depth of this ditch being small, its slopes may be kept very steep. If the wall be more than $4\frac{1}{2}$ feet high, but too low to admit of loop-holes being formed in it, a banquette should be made, to enable the defenders to fire over the wall. The earth for this banquette may be taken from a trench excavated in the rear, in which the troops will be better covered, when not required to man the wall: in front of which a small ditch should be excavated and the earth spread abroad on the ground. Instead of making a banquette, the top of the wall

* *Fr.* Pisé.

may be cut down to form small loop-holes 3 feet apart.

181. *Lofty walls* may be rendered more secure against the effects of the enemy's artillery fire by forming in their rear high and solid banquettes of rubbish, if they are strong enough to support the weight; or two lines of fire may be obtained by forming a banquette of wood work (the tread $4\frac{1}{4}$ feet below the crest of the wall), and piercing loop-holes on the level of the ground. The banquette may be supported on tressels, casks, &c., and be ascended by ladders, or stairs, made with the tables, stools, or other furniture of the neighbouring houses. To enable the defenders to fire through the loop-holes, the external opening of which must be about 3 inches wide, a ditch should be excavated in rear, about $3\frac{1}{2}$ or 4 feet deep, and 2 feet from the wall. In this case no ditch must on any account be made close in front of the wall, as it would serve for cover to the enemy, and enable him to fire through the loop-holes as well as the defenders could.

Fig. 90 represents the arrangements last described, but sometimes the walls may be more completely protected against artillery fire by throwing up more earth in front.

182. When a loop-holed wall is of great extent and in a right line, it would be desirable to flank it by constructing *tambours*, and the wall must

be broken through, to obtain an entrance into the tambours.

The forms of these tambours may be that of a small bastion, or simply of a redan: the salient angle A ought to be 60° (Fig. 91), that the faces AB and AC may give it the most direct flank defence possible. Towards the parts B and C, an oblique direction should be given to the loop-holes of the wall, to obtain a close flanking fire for the faces AB, AC of the tambour. The interior of the tambour may be defended from loop-holes pierced in that part of the wall which it covers.

Tambours are constructed like stoccades with timbers at least 10 feet long, planted touching each other, and sunk 3 feet into the earth. If the tambour is intended to give only one line of fire, the loop-holes must be pierced at the common height of $4\frac{1}{4}$ feet from the ground, and a small ditch excavated in front.

If two lines of fire are wanted, construct a banquette of timber and planks, $4\frac{1}{4}$ feet below the crest of the tambour, then under this banquette pierce loop-holes at the level of the ground. In this case, for the reasons before mentioned, a ditch is to be dug in the interior, and not externally.

Tambours serve also, in certain circumstances, to cover the gates of communication with the exterior; then openings are left between the tambour and the wall, and these passages are closed by barriers, chevaux-de-frise, or loop-holed doors.

If the line of wall were so situated that its prolongation could be taken up by the enemy's artillery, traverses should be thrown up to protect the defenders from enfilade fire; and the flank defences may also be constructed of *earth* in that case.

183. To form *barricades*, anything may be used which can be procured. They may be made with carts sunk up to the axles, and filled with stones and earth; with casks filled in like manner; with trunks of trees, well connected together; with abatis, heaps of stones, rubbish, &c. It frequently happens that the produce of the country furnishes ready means of forming barricades, or even parapets. In South America, the hides collected for exportation were used to form traverses; and in other countries, bales of cotton have been made use of for similar purposes. The best barricades are made with timbers laid across each other, forming square or oblong cases, which may afterwards be filled with earth or stones. A line of waggons placed across a street, with the wheels on one side taken off will be a sufficient impediment to cavalry, if a close musketry fire can be brought to bear on the barricade.

Banquettes should be made in rear of the barricades, to enable the defenders to fire over them;

they may be flanked by loop-holes pierced in the walls of the adjoining houses, and openings should also be made in those walls to enable the defenders to pass round the barricades; a passage may be left between the wall and the end of the traverse or barricade, closed by a barrier-gate; or the barricades may be made to overlap each other so that the barrier will be in a more secure position.

184. It has been stated (art. 176) that an interior intrenchment should if possible be formed, to increase the strength of the post by securing a retreat to the defenders. This intrenchment should be composed of an exterior enclosure and a well-prepared interior post or keep. If the church is to be converted into a keep, the walls of its yard are placed in a state of defence in the manner already described; and in the interior of the church the following arrangements may be made;—The doors and lower windows must be closed up, one entrance only being left; 3-inch plank, or other stout timber, the tiles with which the church is paved, or the tomb-stones, may be used to build up the several openings, leaving loop-holes in the masonry, which will be sufficient to defend the church, if it is built in the form of a cross and some openings are found on each face of the cross; then these loop-holes, though few in number, will, from their flanking each other, be of great value in the defence.

If the building is not built on a plan favourable to flank defence, the loop-holes in the windows will not be sufficient to defend it, for the enemy would then find shelter between them. In this case, loop-holes must be pierced in the walls throughout their whole length.

A tambour should likewise be constructed on each side and end of the building, that every wall may be flanked with the fire of two or three muskets.

185. Another arrangement consists in constructing over ill-flanked doors *machicoulis-galleries*, entered from windows or openings made in the wall for that purpose.

These machicoulis-galleries enable the defenders to fire or throw down shells, grenades, or stones, on the assailants, and thus drive them from the doors, or foot of the wall; of which latter they were the principal defence in ancient fortresses.

The machicoulis-gallery is made to project 2 feet from the wall, in the clear, and has a musket-proof parapet of timber $3\frac{1}{2}$ feet high, Fig. 92. It is supported on brackets, the upper part of each passing through the wall, where it is internally secured to a transverse piece of timber, while the vertical part being applied to the wall prevents the bracket from falling forward. The brackets should be strong, and placed not more than 12 feet apart; they support two sleepers on which the floor is nailed, leaving between the boards spaces equal to their width.

The machicoulis-gallery is commonly placed on the level of the floor, or top of the arch, if the building is vaulted, in order that access to it may be more readily obtained.

Although the arrangement pointed out is sufficiently simple in itself, yet time and means are required for executing it, which cannot always be had.

The following is a substitute for a machicoulis-gallery, which may be made at small expense and with little labour.

Commence by cutting away the wall to such a height that a man may be able to stoop and fire over it from the level of the floor, throughout the whole extent which the machicoulis ought to occupy, Fig. 93; then fasten to the wall with iron cramps, a horizontal piece of timber, *a*, on which nail planks, *b*, placed at distances equal to their width.

These planks should be sufficiently strong to support a piece of scantling, *c*, to which they are nailed; into this piece vertical timbers, *d*, are halved and nailed, and on them three planks are nailed—two on the upper part, and one below, to serve as a parapet for the protection of the troops when throwing stones or grenades, on the assailants, through the openings left between the planks b.

186. If the enemy can, from a distance, destroy the door of a building with his artillery, it may be protected by splinter-proof timbers outside, having one end placed on the ground, and the other against the wall, all touching each other, and then covered with from 5 to 6 feet of earth well rammed, or with earth in sand-bags.

187. Buildings called *blindages* are useful to shelter the troops from the effects of shells in exposed parts; the soldiers find there the repose so necessary after fatiguing duties, or warm and obstinate combats. They are usually constructed by placing strong beams so as to rest at an angle of about 45° against the rear side of a building or traverse, and then covering them with a mass of earth or sand-bags.

In intrenchments intended to last for any length of time, the troops are lodged in a slight kind of blindage, when planks for forming huts cannot be obtained; and these blindages being easily made musket-proof, may be made to serve as defensive barracks. To construct them, excavate the earth 2 feet deep through the extent they are to occupy; stout branches of trees, or rafters, are then fixed across and connected to a ridge-board, kept at its proper height by posts. The branches or rafters are covered with small brushwood or fascines, and a layer of earth about 1 foot thick, over the whole of which a layer of good sod-work is laid

188. When a farm or country-house is to be placed in a state of defence, commence by closing up the windows and barricading the doors. These barricades, which can be overturned at pleasure, enable the defenders to get out of the house, and force through the enemy, if he has blockaded them, so as to make their escape during the night, if deprived of all hope of assistance.

The walls of every floor should be pierced with loop-holes, to which a great depression, must be given, that the enemy while advancing may be as long as possible exposed to the fire from them. The loop-holes on the ground-floor must be pierced $6\frac{1}{2}$ feet above the exterior surface, to prevent the enemy firing into them. The banquette, which may sometimes be necessary to enable the troops to use these loop-holes, may be made with planks supported on trestles, casks, &c. The glass should be removed from the windows, to prevent its fragments injuring the defenders, when it is struck by bullets.

If possible, a loop-hole should be made at every angle of the building, these being the weakest parts; but the cut stone, which is frequently used for the quoins, is an insurmountable impediment when little time is allowed for the completion of the defensive arrangements.

When an external machicoulis-gallery cannot be constructed, holes may at least be made in the roof, through which projectiles of any kind that can be procured may be thrown over on to the enemy.

The building should be unroofed entirely if thatched: it would easily be set fire to if this precaution were not taken, and in the defence of a house nothing is so much to be dreaded: as a protection against it, the floors may be covered with earth or moist dung, and barrels or tubs of water should be placed in every room, the floors being strengthened by posts fixed beneath.

The sleepers and joists which bear on the walls should be shored up, so that, if the enemy batter the house with artillery, the partial fall of the walls may not of necessity be followed by that of the several floors; which, when well supported, may be covered with a sufficient quantity of earth, to render them splinter-proof.

Means of barricading any breach made in the lower part of the building should also be provided, such as branches of trees, timber, casks, bales, or furniture of any kind.

There are few buildings altogether destitute of flank defence, and no opportunity of profiting thereby should on any account be neglected.

189. Behind the barricaded doors, interior retrenchments of wood-work or furniture, &c. are to be made, and openings must be cut in the floors, through which the soldiers may fire down on, or bayonet the assailants; pitchforks, lances, bayonets lashed to poles, or other simple weapons, may be likewise used for their annoyance.

If the house be surrounded by an enclosing wall, it should be prepared for defence in the manner described in art. 180 *et seq.* and all cover inside the enclosure should be removed.

When the premises are very extensive, as may often happen, some parts may be little exposed to attack: in this case the strongest points which command the approaches should be isolated, by destroying the connecting galleries or chambers; thus forming two or more distinct works, either of which may be held, independent of the other.

Of Block-houses.

190. In mountainous, well-wooded countries, block-houses are the best description of defences, because the enemy cannot in these situations, easily bring cannon to attack them, and it is very difficult, in such countries, to find sites for works, free from the defect of being commanded in so great a degree as to render the construction of open works almost useless.

Block-houses are commonly made rectangular,

from 18 to 24 feet wide in the clear; but when they can be made in the form of a cross, Fig. 94, the flanking fire obtained on their faces will render them much more formidable.

A block-house may be liable to be attacked only by infantry, or it may be assailable by artillery; its profile in these two cases should differ.

191. In the first instance, the block-house may be similar to the defensive barrack, described in art. 119, its sides being constructed of logs or squared timbers placed vertically, with loop-holes pierced in them 3 feet apart. The camp-beds serve as banquettes to the loop-holes. They are made $6\frac{1}{2}$ feet wide, with a slope of 10 or 12 inches from the front to the rear. The block-house should be about 20 feet wide, and 9 feet high in the clear; there will then be a free space of 7 feet between the beds. The logs for forming the exterior of the block-house must be from 9 inches to a foot square, and about 12 feet long, so that they may be planted at least 3 feet in the ground. The tops of the logs should have small tenons to fit into a cap-sill morticed to receive them, or they may be placed horizontally one over the other, and halved or notched at the ends to fit close, in the manner in which the log-houses in America are built.

Girders of from 9 to 12 inches square should be halved and bolted into the cap-sill, to prevent the opposite faces of the building from spreading, and to support the roof. The girders must not be placed more than 12 feet apart.

On the girders, joists are laid of from 7 to 9 inches in depth, and 6 or 7 inches apart in the clear; on these joists a floor of planks is laid, and the whole is covered with a layer of earth $1\frac{1}{2}$ or 2 feet thick. To prevent the enemy setting fire to the block-house, a ditch should be dug round it, about 12 feet wide, and 6 feet deep, the earth being partly laid against the block-house to form a parapet, as represented in Fig. 95, and the remainder formed into a small glacis. The scarp of the ditch should be traced at 10 or 12 feet distance from the block-house, to leave room for the base of the parapet. On the glacis, obstacles, such as abatis, shallow military pits, &c., should be placed or formed.

The provisions may be stowed on planks suspended from the ceiling, immediately above the foot of the camp-bed.

192. A block-house to resist the attack of artillery must have two rows of timbers to form the sides, Fig. 96; and the space between the timbers must be filled with earth, well rammed, as high as the loop-holes, making altogether a wall 3 feet thick. These block-houses should be 25 feet wide in the clear, and the girders, formed sometimes of two pieces, may then be connected

together, as in Fig. 98, and be supported by an upright pillar in the centre, standing on a long block of wood, bedded in the ground. The girders should not be more than 6 feet apart, the joists should touch each other, and a floor of planks being laid on them, the whole must be covered with at least $2\frac{1}{2}$ feet of earth.

The width of this block-house is sufficient to allow of a small parapet being constructed on the top, $4\frac{1}{2}$ or 5 feet high, and 3 feet thick. The access to the platform is through a hatchway or trap-door. Under cover of the parapet good marksmen may be posted to fire on the assailants.

The platform above the block-house is of use not only at the moment of attack, but it enables the garrison, if closely blockaded, to get fresh air, cook their victuals, and better discover the enemy's movements.

193. A block-house may be constructed with less timber, by placing the upright timbers 6 or 8 feet apart, against the interior slope of the parapet, and covering them, as before described, with a cap-sill. The men will then fire between the cap-sill and parapet. Fig. 97 represents the exterior elevation of a block-house of this description.

The interior of this block-house would be similar to those already described, excepting that the interior slope of the parapet must be retained with fascines, or stout planks laid on edge, and resting against the upright posts. This arrangement saves wood and labour, but it is less solid, and the defenders are more exposed, both to the weather and to the enemy's fire.

194. When not liable to the attack of artillery, very formidable block-houses may be built two stories in height, the upper story projecting beyond the lower, or with its sides parallel to the diagonals of the lower story, the foot of which may then be well defended by the fire from above. A block-house of this description should be surrounded with a ditch to prevent a near approach.

The advantage of placing the upper story across the lower one is, that there would then be no undefended spaces, and that the enemy could not approach in any direction without being exposed either to the direct fire of one front of the blockhouse, or to a slightly oblique fire of two of its faces.

The timbers forming the sides of a block-house of this description should be laid horizontally one above the other, the ends notched out so as to fit into each other; and the entrance may be effected by a trap-door in the floor of one of the projecting angles.

CHAPTER IX.

ON THE DEFENCE AND ATTACK OF FIELD-WORKS, AND MILITARY POSTS.

On the Defence.

195. HAVING explained the principles to be observed in tracing and constructing the various intrenchments which may be thrown up in the field, and shown the arrangements necesssary to be made, and the means to be employed for augmenting the strength of military posts, it now becomes necessary to point out some of the rules to be observed in guarding and defending, or in attacking, those intrenchments or posts. It has often happened that the vigorous defence of a military post, the possession of which might originally have appeared to be of little consequence, has either secured an army from entire defeat, or ensured its ultimate success,

The defenders of a post may be beaten, but they ought never to be found off their guard: their courage is put in requisition to prevent a defeat, their vigilance to avert a surprise; but neither their courage nor vigilance will much avail, unless both are skilfully directed.

Although the break of day is the moment when

the vigilance of a commanding officer is most necessary, he ought not on that account to pass the remainder of his time in a state of inactivity: the soldiers under his authority would soon follow his example, and the enemy, informed of his negligence would regulate their hour of attack accordingly, with every prospect of success.

Not to fatigue the troops too much, they should be divided into four reliefs, so as to take the duty by turns.

One relief is held in readiness for action, and is employed in improving the defences: a second furnishes guards and patrols; the two others repose.

To Guard and Defend an Earthen Work.

196. The first care of an officer in command of a detachment sent to occupy a work, is that of placing his sentries, both in the interior and externally. A sentry should be placed in the interior at each of the salient angles of the work, and externally to guard each of the avenues by which an enemy might approach, principally on the side next him, but not neglecting to place some sentries to watch the approaches on the other sides; for the enemy might pass round the post with a view to take it by surprise.

If in front of the work there be a bridge, a causeway, a defile, or a ford, over or through which the enemy is compelled to pass, and which can neither be destroyed nor occupied—if there be any house, or hollow road, or ravine, in which he might conceal troops, a few intelligent and trustworthy men should be placed to watch those points, and to give timely notice of the enemy's movements.

In general, the sentries are most numerously posted on those sides of the work easiest of access to the enemy. They should always have particular instructions given them as to their conduct in the event of an attack either on the side they guard, or on any other point.

The patrols sent out to ascertain whether the sentries are on the alert, or to reconnoitre the enemy, should be taught that they are not sent to fight, but to inspect carefully the hollow ways, hedges, ditches, woods, and houses, in the neighbourhood, and to give information of what they may discover to the officer in charge of the post.

But if a patrol accidentally encounter any small party of the enemy, they should attack them instantly with the bayonet, and drive them as far off as possible.

If the patrol fall in with an ambuscade, they should instantly fire on them, however superior their numbers, in order to awaken the vigilance of any party of their comrades who may be approaching.

These precautions, and others which circumstances will suggest, may be sufficient to prevent the enemy either surprising or reconnoitring a post.

Intelligence as to the enemy's numbers, position, preparations, &c. may often be obtained from the peasantry of the country; but these sources of information are always liable to suspicion; for the enemy may bribe some of the natives to give false intelligence, or may cause persons in his service to spread rumours of such import as he would wish to be believed.

After having taken the precautions already mentioned against surprise, the commandant of the post should next prepare his measures of defence, and point out to his detachment their respective duties, under the several circumstances to which an attack may give rise. He will instruct them not to approach the parapet, or to fire until the enemy is within range.

197. The moment the enemy makes his appearance, the commanding officer should order the detachment to stand to their arms, and send a messenger to the general, or other commanding officer of the troops in the neighbourhood. He should then inspect every part of the work, to see that his previous orders have been strictly adhered to, and that every one is at his assigned post.

If the enemy make a breach with his artillery, it should be closed with limbs of trees, chevaux-de-frise, planks with spikes driven through them, crows' feet, or other impediments previously collected in the interior of the work for this purpose.

The reserve should be posted near the centre of the work, ready to give assistance wherever the assailants are on the point of effecting an entrance.

We have supposed the enemy to have attacked all the assailable points at the same moment; but if the attack were only partial, then the parts attacked would be reinforced by the troops originally posted to defend the other faces.

The defenders should endeavour to distinguish the true from the feigned attacks; for a skilful antagonist usually makes several, particularly during the night, and these false or true attacks often change their object, according to the degree of resistance they may happen to meet with.

If, after having valiantly defended a post, no aid can be expected, and the garrison are reduced to the last extremity, they should endeavour to escape during the night. The commandant of a post should, however, never forget that this is to be his last resource; and that, however unimportant the work may appear, the prolongation of its defence for only a quarter of an hour may perhaps save an entire division or corps.

Manner of Guarding and Defending a Church, a Country-Seat, or a House. *

198. What has been alread stated with regard to vigilance, and the posting of sentries, &c., is equally applicable to the defence of churches, farmhouses, or other buildings.

These edifices being secured from surprise, the preparatory arrangements for their defence are to be made

The commandant of the post should divide his troops into as many parties as there are floors to be occupied, placing one or two men to defend each window and overturn any ladders the enemy may plant, to scale the walls.

Two men should be posted at each window or loop-hole on the ground-floor: one man will be sufficient to defend each loop-hole on the upper floors.

After having made as great a resistance as possible on the ground floor, the defenders may be forced to mount to the first floor, drawing up their ladders after them. They then keep up the heaviest fire possible on the enemy below, through loop-holes made in the floor for this purpose. If the assailants commence collecting combustible

* Large public buildings and institutions, such as the county gaols of this country, are generally admirably calculated for defence; and it is only to be regretted that they are not invariably constructed with flank defences.

material to burn the house, they should endeavour to wet them. If the enemy endeavours to undermine the walls, burst open the doors, or enter at the windows, heavy blocks of wet timber, stones, bricks, or other materials, should be thrown on him; taking care not to make too liberal a use of these means of defence during the first efforts of the enemy, and thus to exhaust your supply, before the attack has assumed its most formidable aspect.

In defending a house, it would rarely be advisable to make sorties, because the narrowness of the passages through which the troops would have to file would prevent your showing the enemy a good front, or making a secure retreat in case of necessity.

Manner of Guarding and Defending an Intrenched Village.

199. After having provided for the security of the village, by taking the proper measures to prevent a surprise, the commandant should place a guard in the house or church occupied as an interior intrenchment, and another at the spot where the reserve is to be posted. These different guards should have a ready and secure communication with each other.

If cavalry form part of the force, some small detachments should be kept on the outside of the fortified enclosure, their object being to patrol the neighbourhood, especially on the side of the enemy. At night, these are to be replaced by small detachments of infantry, who perform the duties already pointed out for the advanced posts.

Each detachment should have with them one or two horsemen, who may speedily communicate to the commandant information of any discoveries made by the patrols in the execution of their duties.

If the position is intersected by a small river, the points where it enters and leaves the village should be carefully guarded. To keep the detachment on the alert, and in order to ascertain whether every one knows his post, an alarm may occasionally be given. These alarms should not, however, be often repeated; one or two will be sufficient to show whether your troops know their duty, and execute it promptly; more are unnecessary, as they would only harass the men, and perhaps make those negligent who would otherwise have been all activity.

During the attack, the cavalry should be kept in readiness in the immediate vicinity of the point attacked; or if several attacks be made, in the market-place, or other favourable position, from which they can proceed to charge the enemy with vigour whenever he may penetrate into the village

When the enemy has surmounted the obstacles, presented to him, such as abatis, pits, &c., the garrison, if sufficiently numerous, should make a sortie on one or both of his flanks. A well-timed offensive movement can seldom fail to throw him into disorder, because he would immediately imagine that he is assaulting a much more powerful garrison than he had previously supposed, as it would appear to him that otherwise they would not have ventured, by assuming the offensive, to place themselves on an equality with the assailants.

In defending a military post, sorties should not be made until the time when the enemy is about to scale the parapet, or when he has been thrown into disorder by the fire of the defenders.

If a military post be blockaded by an enemy, a sortie may sometimes be required to attract his attention, while reinforcements of men, ammunition, or provisions, are arriving.

200. Sorties during an assault should always be powerful, and therefore can only be made when an extensive post is occupied in sufficient force to be defended with the greatest possible vigour. Those made by small numbers will seldom or never produce an effect equivalent to the certain disadvantage of being immediately beaten back.

The commandant of an extensive post, should never lead a sortie, except for the purpose of opening a passage through the enemy to escape. He should not let his courage get the better of his judgment, nor unneccessarily expose his life until he feels himself called on to set an example.

The troops intended for a sortie should be placed near the points of exit; they march at a given signal, when the fire from the adjacent intrenchments must cease. They are not to halt, or commence firing, but proceed at once to use the bayonet. Having effected their object, they are immediately to return at a rapid pace, the reserve being held in readiness to support the retreat if necessary, and the parapets near the barriers being well manned, so as to pour in a heavy fire upon the enemy if he attempts to follow.

If the post be so strongly intrenched as to compel the enemy to cannonade it, a second line of defence may be prepared, as soon as his arrangements indicate on what part of the post he intends to direct his attack.

It is supposed that the streets have already been well barricaded, the walls of the houses loopholed, &c.; what may be done now is, to barricade the space between the houses and the outer enclosure, either with an abatis or any other impediments, in order that if the enemy get possession of any parts, his lateral movements may be efficiently obstructed.

When the defenders can no longer resist the

attack directed against the outer defences, they must retire to the interior intrenchment, where they will continue to defend themselves in such manner as the means there provided will permit.

On the Attack.

201. The manner of attacking field-works is very different from that employed in the attack of fortresses.

In the attack of field-works the assailants are always more or less exposed to view, whilst in that of fortresses, their approaches are made by excavating trenches, the bottoms of which form the road by which they advance, and the earth excavated being thrown towards the place protects them from its fire.

An officer charged with the attack of a military post should first endeavour to procure—from plans of the country—from a careful reconnoissance, and from spies, a knowledge of the nature of the ground occupied by the post—the various roads by which it may be approached—the description of works thrown up for the defence—the number and description of troops opposed to him—the quantity of ammunition, provisions, &c., with which they are supplied—the manner in which the military duties are performed—the disposition and habits of the commanding officer—the probable succour the post may receive, and how long it must hold out in order to benefit by that aid.

If the post be only a church or a farm-house, he should, if possible, find out what internal arrangements have been made, how the doors, windows, and different floors are defended, whether loop-holes have been pierced in the walls and floors whether tambours have been made, and ditches excavated, &c.

If the post be an intrenched village, he must endeavour to learn what avenues the enemy has closed, and in what manner it has been done, how the houses skirting the village have been fortified, and what building has been selected for the interior redoubt.

There are three methods of attack, distinguished as attacks *by surprise, stratagem, or force.*

Attacks by Surprise.

202. To succeed in an attack by surprise, it is desirable to deceive the enemy by making such arrangements as would lead him to imagine that some totally different enterprise was meditated.

The winter is the most favourable season for executing such attacks, and on rainy nights sentries are least on the alert. They are usually commenced about two hours before day-light; and the march of the troops should be so regulated that they may arrive in the neighbourhood at that time.

If the post to be surprised can be readily succoured, the attack should be made early enough to allow of the enterprise being completed, and a retreat commenced, if necessary, before the dawn of day, if, as is here supposed, the force which can be brought in aid of the garrison be more numerous than the attacking corps; and an attack must not be commenced before the garrison and inhabitants have retired to rest; consequently not much before midnight.

The strength of the detachment employed in the attack is to be proportioned to that of the garrison, and of the corps whose aid they may probably obtain, the number of defiles or passes it may be necessary to occupy, (in order to secure a retreat,) and of true or false attacks intended to be made.

203. The men who undertake a surprise may be divided into four parties: 1st, the attacking party; 2nd, that for false attacks; 3rd, the troops to support them, and to cover their retreat; 4th, the working party.

Guides and interpreters should be attached to each party; but before the care of conducting the different detachments is confided to the guides, it must be ascertained that their knowledge is sufficiently perfect to enable them to fulfil their obligations. They should be promised an ample remuneration if they do their duty faithfully, and certain death if they mislead, or in any other manner attempt to deceive.

Each detachment should be led by an officer of Engineers who has reconnoitred the works, and should be accompanied by two guides, so that if one be killed or wounded, another may be ready to take his place.

The troops should never be allowed to fire in making an attack by surprise, but must endeavour to surmount every obstacle silently, until they can contend hand to hand with the enemy.

Bags made either of leather or canvass, filled with powder, and having a fuze attached, must be provided for bursting open gates or barriers, and blowing up wooden bridges. The bag of powder is to be suspended to, or propped against the woodwork, in the readiest manner that offers, and a gimlet should be carried with the bag for this purpose.

Strong pincers, heavy hammers, and iron wedges are also required for breaking open the barriers, knocking off the locks, or removing the hinges of the gates. Hand-saws and axes are carried for cutting the fraises, palisades, and barriers; shovels and pick-axes to cut away the crest of the counterscarp so as to render its descent more easy, and form openings in the intrenchments; steel spikes to spike the guns; and ladders to scale the stoccades, garden-walls, &c.

After having made provision for the several objects above specified, the commanding officer, when the attack is on a large scale, may subdivide his detachment thus :—one portion to execute the true attack, a second to make two or three false attacks, a third to oppose the party sent in aid of the garrison, or to create a diversion by attacking some other part of the enemy's position, a fourth to form a reserve, and a fifth to guard the defiles and cover the retreat. This supposes the projected attack to be made with numerous forces against a formidable adversary, intrenched in an extensive position.

In some cases, however, a body of troops might not be required to cover the retreat. This is only mentioned, therefore, by way of example; for, generally, the troops to cover the retreat are independent of the attacking corps.

It is not possible to say what proportions these several detachments should bear one to another; that destined for the true attack must not, however, be less than one-third of the garrison; those for the false attacks should also be considerable, otherwise they would be unable to take advantage of any unexpected success on their parts.

The corps to oppose the expected succour, and that left to guard the defiles, &c., should be proportioned, the one to the probable number of troops which may be detached in aid of the post, the other to the number and capabilities of defence of the defiles they may have to occupy, and the distance between the assailants and their point of departure.

The reserve should be the most numerous body, and, if possible, be composed of old soldiers. They ought to be placed in such a position, with reference to the true and false attacks, that they may give assistance to whichever party first penetrates the enemy's intrenchments.

When the officer commanding the principal attack approaches the counterscarp, he should push forward the party who carry the scaling ladders, which party must consist of two divisions: the first lower their ladders into the ditch, descend the counterscarp, and place the same ladders against the scarp: the second division lower their ladders, and descending into the ditch, are immediately followed by the remainder of the storming party. Plenty of ladders should be employed, to provide for the loss of some, and to obtain a large front for the assaulting column.

If the men who first ascend are perceived, instead of replying to the challenge, they must rush quietly towards the sentries, and endeavour either to secure them without noise, or bayonet them.

When the post is surrounded by a wet ditch, fascines, 6 feet in length, are to be thrown into it, to form a bridge; or if the bottom of the ditch be soft and muddy, it must be covered with hurdles prepared for that purpose. The rear divisions of each attack, who in the first instance remain in silence near the counterscarp, follow the first division as soon as it has entered the place.

A detachment should be posted to guard internally the point by which the intrenchments have been penetrated, otherwise the enemy might get possession of it, and prevent any further assistance being given to those who first entered the work.

The detachment which first gets within the enemy's intrenchments should proceed immediately to spike the guns and facilitate the nearest attacks on their flanks.

Another should march towards the point indicated for the entrance of the reserve, and open a way for them.

As soon as the reserve has been introduced, any further orders which may have been given are executed, and each party should repair immediately to the appointed place of general rendezvous. The first object to be attended to, after getting possession of the post, is to secure the persons of the commanding officer and of the principal magistrates.

The true attack should be made at a point where the houses are most distant from the intrenchment, where the enclosure is feebly guarded, or where it is not secured by a ditch; in short, the principal attack must be directed against the weakest point of the enemy's post; while, on the contrary, one of the false attacks should be made against the strongest part of the works where the enemy have least cause to expect an assault.

Although the detachment sent to oppose the arrival of aid, may not have given any intimation of the enemy's approach, the commanding officer must not on that account neglect to take such measures as the nature of the situation requires, to render the arrival of that aid unavailing.

When it is intended to retain the post, he will proceed immediately to adopt all those means of defence described in the preceding parts of this treatise. When, on the contrary, it is to be abandoned, he will destroy the ammunition, guns and magazines, fill in the ditches, set fire to the abatis, and break down the palisades, fraises, dams, &c., before he commences his retreat.

In the rules above detailed, it has been supposed that every measure has had a fortunate result; but numerous obstacles may be opposed to that success by a viligant and intelligent opponent; it is necessary, therefore, to consider well the different unfavourable circumstances which might arise, and to instruct the officers in charge of the several detachments as to the measures they are to take in the event of a failure in one attack, or success in another.

Attacks by Stratagem.

204. It is unnecessary to say much on the subject of attacks by stratagem, because what has been already stated with respect to attacks by surprise is equally applicable to them: secrecy is their soul, and prudence should be observed in the arrangements made for their execution. An active foresight will generally enable the assailant to avoid unnecessary dangers: you should give the enemy credit for doing his duty properly, and your measures being taken accordingly, a successful termination to the enterprise may be confidently anticipated.

By obtaining the co-operation of some inhabitants, an officer may frequently succeed in introducing himself into a post: in treating with them, he should never forget, however, that he is leagued with rogues, who will not hesitate to sacrifice him, if necessary to their own interest.

Circumstances give rise to stratagems, yet these stratagems have bounds; and although we may be justified in deceiving an enemy by every possible artifice, and laying any snare to entrap him, yet all perfidy is disgraceful, and is forbidden by the laws of honour.

Attacks by Open Force.

205. Before an officer undertakes to carry a

post by open force, he should acquire all the information respecting it detailed in the preceding articles. Every attack requires that he who directs it should be perfectly well acquainted with the nature of the ground on which he is to manœuvre, and should have made a close examination of the situation, and of its strong and weak points; for the first arrangements of the attack are always in a great measure dictated by those of the enemy. The rules given for attacks by surprise are also applicable to those by open force. Both require the formation of several attacks, some true, others feigned. These attacks must all commence at the same moment; and if any of the assailing columns have to make a circuit to get opposite their points of attack, they should be informed exactly at what hour they are to give the assault; and plenty of time must be allowed for their march.

Works of slight profile, or weakly garrisoned, may often be carried by a sudden assault, which should be made just before day-break. If the attack is commenced during day-light; when the troops are in readiness to march, a few detachments of light infantry may be pushed forward to attract the fire of the defenders from the real point of attack, while at the same time the main body of infantry advance with speed, and charge with vigour; and the artillery enfilade and shell the works bearing upon the lines of approach.

Every attack should be formidable in point of numbers that the enemy may have real cause for apprehension from each of them.

The enemy should be kept in check during the attack, and be prevented from reinforcing the works or manœuvring on the flanks of the assailing columns.

An assault cannot be too rapidly given. A rapid advance raises the spirits of the assailants, and prevents their loss from the fire of the defenders being so great as it would be if they were exposed to it for a longer period.

The assaulting column must on no account stop to fire, but firing parties should be appointed, specially to keep down both the artillery and musketry fire of the defenders. The attacking columns should have supports close at hand, and should be so directed that they may succour each other, and be prepared to repel sorties.

A military post may be well defended without artillery, but a strongly intrenched position can seldom be carried by open force if the assailants are unprovided with cannon.

When the scarps cannot be ascended without ladders and none can be procured, a work may sometimes be entered by mining them, if unflanked, or by enlarging any partial breach. The sappers who first descend into the ditch, in this case, carry with them crowbars, pick-axes, and shovels,

&c.; and as soon as they have made a practicable passage, they enter the post, followed by the remainder of the detachment. When the assailants are furnished with artillery, it should be placed so as to obtain a slanting fire against walls exposed to be breached.

A redoubt even of a good profile, may be assaulted in the following manner:—At dawn some artillery should gallop up, unlimber, and commence a rapid fire to drive the defenders from the parapets, enfilading them if possible; a working party carrying fascines, followed by a powerful storming party, advance at the same time with the greatest possible speed; and the former fill up the ditch enough to enable the latter to cross it and enter the work.

Attacks by open force should generally be preceded by a ricochet fire with shells, and the works should be attacked by the gorge or rear faces, as well as in front, if possible.

When compelled to breach a work with artillery before assaulting it, a small epaulment may be thrown up, with gabions to protect the guns; or, if the site permit, a terreplein may be excavated for them, and a parapet formed in front.

206. The means of giving to works the greatest degree of strength of which they may be susceptible have already been described. It now remains to show in what manner an officer should

overcome the obstacles usually found in a strongly intrenched position.

An abatis, if not properly covered, may be destroyed by artillery, placing the guns so as to enfilade it, and using ricochet fire. Howitzers are the description of ordnance best adapted for effecting breaches in earthen works, or destroying kaponiers, fraises, palisading, or abatis, &c.

To burn an abatis, lighted faggots may be thrown on it, but no troops can pass it till the fire has burnt out.

Crows' feet may be swept away during the night with branches of trees, which the men drag after them.

If military pits are to be crossed, the men must march in extended order, and at a slow pace; and sometimes they may be filled up with bundles of hay or covered over with planks.

Palisades and Chevaux-de-frise should, if possible, first be broken by the fire of artillery, then a few resolute sappers with axes are sent forward to open a passage through them; the fire of the flanking works being kept down as much as possible whilst they are doing this.

Breaches may also be made in palisades and kaponiers by attaching bags of powder to them, and exploding them as explained in art. 234, and stoccades may be set fire to with red hot shot.

The best method of destroying fraises is to enfilade them with artillery; gaps will then be made of sufficient magnitude to permit of their demolition being completed with axes; or they may be destroyed with powder in the manner alluded to in the last paragraph.

In the attack of fortified houses, the fire from them may sometimes be stopped by the introduction of small rockets, or any other fire-work that will create an abundance of smoke.

The walls of a house may be breached by undermining them, or by artillery placed so as to hit them obliquely; a very few shot taking effect near an angle of the building will then bring them down. If the house is to be carried by escalade, it must be attacked on several points at the same moment; parties being posted under cover, to keep up a steady fire on such of the defenders as may show themselves, and especially to silence the *flanking* fire. If the upper floors are gained, hand-grenades, pitched faggots, and lighted torches &c., should be thrown into it.

Churches are attacked in the same manner as common houses; but, the walls being usually much thicker, the attack would probably not succeed unless they were previously breached by heavy artillery.

When the enemy's fortifications are of so perfect a nature as to render hopeless any attempt to carry them by open force, the method of attack detailed in the 11th chapter of this treatise must be resorted to. Though the planning and directing attacks of this description would generally be referred to an experienced officer of engineers, of whose duties in the field this forms an important part, yet all military officers ought to understand the principles on which this kind of attack is founded, the description and use of the several intrenchments, batteries, &c., thrown up; and so much of the detail as will enable them, in a case of emergency, to proceed with the work, commenced under the direction of the engineer.

CHAPTER X.

MILITARY MINING.

Dimensions of Galleries and Branches.

207. In attacking, defending, and demolishing works, it is often necessary to explode charges of powder underground; in order to place these, small tunnels (called *galleries* and *branches*, according to their dimensions), are required to be constructed, and vertical excavations, called *shafts*, are also necessary for the same purpose. The following dimensions are commonly given to the galleries and branches of mines:—

Description of Gallery or Branch.	Height in the clear.				Breadth in the clear.			
	′	″	′	″	′	″	′	″
Great gallery used for descents into ditches &c.	6	0	to 6	6	5	0	to 7	6
Common Gallery . . .	4	3	5	0	3	3	3	6
Branch	3	0	3	6	2	6	2	9

The galleries and branches in permanent works are constructed of masonry. In works of a temporary nature the earth at the top and sides is supported by *frames* of wood and planks called *sheeting*, or by *cases*.

Each frame consists of four pieces, viz., a ground-sill, two stanchions, and a cap-sill. These pieces are connected together at the ends by notches cut in each, Fig. 99, an inch and a half in depth. The following table shows the scantling for gallery frames, supposing the earth to be of a medium consistency, and the wood to be well-seasoned oak :—

Description of Gallery or Branch.	Ground-sill.	Stanchions	Cap-sill.
	" "	" "	" "
Great Gallery . . .	6 × 4½	6 × 6	7 × 6
Common Gallery. .	4½ × 3½	4½ × 4½	5 × 4½
Branch	3½ × 3	3½ × 3½	4½ × 3½

The top sheeting is from 3 feet 6 inches to 4 feet long, from 7 inches to 1 foot wide, and from 1 inch to 1½ inches thick. The side sheeting should be from ¾ of an inch to 1 inch thick.

The frames are connected together by battens, 2½ to 3 inches wide, and 1 inch thick.

Gallery frames and sheeting are not much used now at the Establishment for the instruction of the Engineers at Chatham, as cases, which consist of planks only, are considered more convenient (see Art. 214), Figure 117.

The dimensions of the cases now in use are

Description of Gallery or Branch.	Height in the clear.		Width in the clear.		Thickness.
	′	″	′	″	
Great Gallery . . .	6	6	7	6	4
Gallery	4	6	3	0	2
Branch	3	6	2	6	2

The cases for shafts are 4′ 6″ by 3′ 6″, and 2 inches thick.

When great galleries are driven so as to descend into a ditch, either under, or near to a breaching battery, some additional thickness will be required to be given to the cap sills and stanchions.

Construction of Shafts.

208. When a gallery is to be driven from the bottom of a shaft, the greatest width of the shaft in the clear must be at least equal to that of the gallery from out to out.

When a shaft is sunk merely for the purpose of demolition, it should be made as small as possible. A shaft 3 feet by 2 feet is the smallest in which a miner can conveniently work after sinking 6 feet in depth.

Two kinds of frames are used for shafts, viz., top frames and side frames.

The top frame consists of four pieces, halved to fit each other, with an overlength of from $1\frac{1}{2}$ to 2 feet, Fig. 100. The side frames also consist of four pieces, the ends halved to fit one another, Fig. 101. Each piece of the shaft-frame has a line or score cut with a saw on all its faces, marking the middle of the piece.

The scantling for the top frames of a shaft should generally be larger than for the side frames, the former being 6 inches and the latter $5\frac{1}{3}$ inches square.

When the shaft is less than 4 feet 4 inches wide in the clear, the scantling may be reduced.

If it were required to drive a gallery from the bottom of a shaft, the distance of the floor of the gallery below the surface of the ground being given, the first thing to be done is to determine the length of the intervals.

An interval of a shaft or gallery is the vertical or horizontal distance between two frames, added to the thickness of a frame.

To find the lengths of the intervals, let us suppose that a common gallery 4 feet 6 inches high in the clear is to be driven from the bottom of a shaft 22 feet deep.

To find the height of the lowest frame above the bottom we then have—

	′	″
Height of the gallery from the top of the ground-sill to the top of the cap-sill	4	11
Thickness of the top sheeting	0	1
Free space for the introduction of the top sheeting .	0	2
Thickness of the shaft-frame next above the gallery	0	4½
Total . . .	5	6½

Subtract 5 feet 6½ inches from the total depth of 22 feet, there remains 16 feet 5½ inches above it.

There would then be four intervals of 3 feet 4 inches each, and one of 3 feet 2½ inches, Fig. 102.

In sinking the shaft, the frames are connected together by battens, similar to those described in art. 207, their length being equal to that of an interval added to the thickness of a shaft-frame.

These battens are nailed to the shaft-frames 4 inches from their halvings, on the opposite sides of the shaft, two pieces of the frame being thus suspended by them, with the halvings turned upwards; the other two pieces are fitted on the first, and to these the battens of the next interval are nailed: so that if (Fig. 100) the battens of the first interval were nailed to the pieces 1 and 3, those of the second interval would be nailed to the pieces of the shaft frame next below 2 and 4.

Having determined the length of the intervals, three pickets are to be driven into the ground 9 or 10 feet apart, one to mark the centre of the shaft, the others to shew the direction of the axis or central line of the intended gallery. The top frame of the shaft is then let into the ground, taking care that it is perfectly level, that the semi-diagonals measured from the central picket are all equal, and that the scores of two opposite pieces of the frame are laid exactly in the direction of the axis of the gallery marked by three pickets previously driven.

The ends of the top frame should be secured with pickets, driving them at both ends of each piece at the same time. When the ground is irregular a level berth for the top frame must be excavated. In favourable soil it may not be necessary to introduce more than two or three pieces of sheeting on each side of the shaft, after the interval has been excavated, and the first frame of the next interval has been placed. In unfavourable soil, on the contrary, the sheeting must be introduced behind the frames, after excavating only a portion of the interval; in this case a false or temporary frame is used to keep the sheeting in its place. The false frame is similar to the side frames, but a little larger in the clear. The manner of using it is sufficiently explained by Fig. 103.

In sinking the shaft care must be taken, that all the scores of the frames on each side lie in a vertical line.

Construction of Galleries.

209. When the shaft is sunk to its proper depth, a central picket is to be driven at the bottom, to mark the direction of the axis of the gallery.

In favourable soil the sheeting on that side of the last interval from which the gallery is to be driven may be dispensed with, and the first frame of the gallery may be placed on the outside of the shaft, as represented in Fig. 104.

In unfavourable soil the whole shaft must be lined with sheeting, a frame being introduced in the middle of the last interval, Fig. 105.

* The first frame of the gallery is then set up within the shaft, and the stanchions are secured with battens to the intermediate shaft-frame of the last interval. The sheeting opposite to the cap-sill of the first gallery-frame is then forced down with a crow-bar, until sufficient room is obtained to introduce the top-sheeting of the gallery

---

* *Cases* are now generally used for shafts and galleries, but as there is no material difference in the mode of proceeding whether frames or cases are used, the description of the manner in which the work is done when frames and sheeting are used is here given; even with cases a frame is required to be fixed at the commencement of a gallery, to keep the cases of the shaft from collapsing when the pieces are removed to allow of an opening being made for it.

and one or two pieces of the side sheeting. A piece of timber is placed across the shaft under the frame next above the gallery, to take the ends of the top sheeting; and the side sheeting, if necessary, must be counter-supported in a similar manner against the sides of the shaft. When the side sheeting has been introduced as far down as the intermediate shaft-frame, that piece of it which extends across the gallery is lifted off the side ones, between which and the stanchions wedges must be previously driven.

210. The top sheeting of the gallery should always be driven as the excavation is advanced; the rear ends of the sheeting being kept down with wedges introduced between it and the top sheeting of the last interval. The thickness of these wedges should be diminished as the work advances.

When the floor of the gallery is level, the battens to secure the stanchions to each other should be nailed alternately 4 and 8 inches below the cap-sill. In ascending and descending galleries, the battens are nailed 4 inches below the lowest cap-sill of each interval, and 4 inches more than the thickness of the slope-block below the highest cap-sill of each interval; they are thus kept level without trouble.

The slope-block is a cube of wood, the side of the cube being made equal to the intended difference of level between the two frames of an interval.

In unfavourable soil a false frame is introduced in the middle of each interval, to take the ends of the sheeting. The false frame, Fig. 106, is a little shorter and wider than the gallery-frames, the cap-sill is rounded at the top, the stanchions have small tenons at their upper ends, which are let into mortices cut in the cap-sill; these mortices are longer than the tenons, a wedge is therefore introduced to keep the stanchions in their places. When the wedge is drawn out, the frame is easily removed: but this is not to be done until the second frame of the interval is put up, and wedges are introduced between it and the sheeting to facilitate the introduction of the sheeting of the next interval.

211. In a descending gallery, the frames, instead of being placed vertically, should be set up perpendicular to the slope; more head-room is thus obtained, and the work can be executed with greater facility. This is the mode adopted at the practical school at Chatham; but the French miners always place the frames perpendicular to the horizon.

Returns in Galleries.

212. When the axes of two galleries meet at a

given point, or a change of direction is made in the axis of a gallery, it is called a *return*.

The interval in which the return is made, is called a *landing*, and must always be level.

When the return is to be made at right angles with the original gallery, called the *gallery of departure*, the distance apart of the frames at that point must be so regulated that the front of the first frame of the landing may be at a distance from the point of intersection of the axes of the return and gallery of departure, equal to half the width of the return from out to out; the length of the whole landing in the clear being equal to twice that distance, Fig. 107.

If the return form with the gallery of departure an angle greater than 45°, a tracing of the return, similar to Fig. 108, should be made on a floor, in order to determine the exact dimensions of the oblique frame, and the distances required to be known for setting it up accurately.

When the axis of the return forms an angle of less than 45° with that of the gallery of departure, two returns must be made, the first at right angles, the second oblique, as shewn in Fig. 109. If the return is to be made entirely with square frames, then a small recess, A, Fig. 110, must be excavated to obtain room for the introduction of the sheeting of the return.

When the gallery of departure is not prolonged

beyond the return, the frames must be arranged as in Fig. 111.

In favourable soil, when the angle of the return is not less than 60°, the frames may be placed as in Fig. 112.

To find the Length of the Intervals of a Gallery.

213. The length of the intervals of a gallery, usually about $2\frac{1}{2}$ feet, should evidently be determined before its execution is commenced; but we have deferred explaining this operation, in order that the preceding details may make it more intelligible.

The officer in charge should first determine, by means of a tracing on the ground, and by levelling, the different horizontal and vertical lengths required to be known.

Given AB the axis of a gallery, its length being 118 feet, Fig. 113. A shaft is sunk at the point A; at the point C, situated 44 feet from A, there is to be a common gallery at right angles to the gallery of departure; at the point D, 44 feet from C, there is to be an oblique return of a great branch, forming with the gallery of departure an angle of 45°.

The part AC is a common great gallery; the part CD a common gallery; and the part DB a branch.

The levels of the points AC, DB, referred to the same comparative plane, passing above all of them, are,

		′	″
For the point A	. .	34	0
,, C	. .	29	0
,, D	. .	33	1
,, B	. .	35	1

Thus, from A to C there is an ascent of 5 feet; from C to D a descent of 4 feet; from D to B a descent of 2 feet.

Part AC, Fig. 114. From the entire length of this part, 44 feet, subtract

	′	″
Half the width in the clear of the shaft . .	2	2
The thickness of the lower shaft frame . .	0	4¼
Half the width of the landing at C . . .	2	0¼
The thickness of the last ground-sill of the gallery AC	0	5
	5	0

There will then remain 39 feet, which gives twelve intervals, each one 3 feet 4 inches in length. In these twelve intervals the gallery has to ascend 5 feet, consequently the side of the slope block will be 5 inches.

Part CD, Fig. 115.—Having constructed the plan of the oblique return to be executed at D, we find that the last frame of CD is to be distant, say 9 inches, from the point D. Then, from the whole distance CD, 44 feet, subtract

FIELD FORTIFICATION. 211

	'	"
The half breadth of the landing C . .	2	0½
The thickness of the gallery-frame placed beyond point C	0	
The distance of the point D from the last frame .	0	9
The thickness of the last frame of the gallery CD	0	4½
	3	7

There remains 40 feet 5 inches, which gives thirteen intervals, nine of 3 feet 1 inch, and four of 3 feet 2 inches. The side of the slope-block will be 3 inches.

Part DB, Fig. 116.—Measure on the plan of the oblique return the distance of the point D from the rear of the frame placed beyond it, to form the landing. We will suppose that this distance is found to be 4 feet 5 inches; then from the whole length of the part DB, 30 feet, subtract

	'	"
The distance above given	4	5
The thickness of the great branch-frame placed beyond D	0	3½
The thickness of the last frame placed at B .	0	3½
	5	0

There remains 25 feet, or six intervals of 3 feet 2 inches each, and two of 3 feet, the side of the slope-block being 3 inches.

Shafts and Galleries lined with Cases.

214. The dimensions of these are given in Art. 207; the cases are made of plank, about 11 inches wide and 2 inches thick, except those for

great galleries which require to be about 4 inches thick. They may be fixed at intervals, greater or less according to the nature of the soil, or touching each other; and they serve at the same time both as frames and sheeting.

Each case consists of four pieces; the stanchions have a tenon at each end, Fig. 117, fitting into mortices or notches cut in the cap-sill and ground-sill to receive them.

When the gallery is an ascending or descending one, the ends of the stanchions are sometimes cut obliquely, in order that their sides may always be vertical, see Fig. 117.

Fig. 118 is a plan and section of this description of gallery, the construction of which is so simple that it can be executed more rapidly than that formed with frames.

Shafts à la Boule.

215. These shafts are lined with cases made of plank, connected together as shewn in Fig. 119.

In Fig. 120 a section of a shaft *à la Boule*, is shewn, which is sufficiently explanatory to render any other description unnecessary.

This kind of shaft can only be used with advantage in favourable soil, on account of the difficulty of introducing the cases sufficiently near each other; they are commonly placed 1 foot apart, as shewn in the figure. Large gabions, 6 feet long, and from 3 feet 6 inches to 4 feet in diameter, are sometimes used for lining shafts near the surface.

Of Mine Chambers.

216. The chamber of a mine is a cavity formed in any place to receive a charge of powder, intended to be there exploded.

When the chamber is to be near the end of a gallery, a small return is made to receive the charge. When the charge is not required to be exploded immediately, or the ground is much saturated with moisture, it must be placed in a well-pitched wooden case: a good cask might be employed, or the wooden case may be covered with tarpaulin, but the safest plan is to place the charge in water-tight tin cases.

In dry ground, and when the charge is to be exploded in a short time, it may be contained in tarred bags.

When the case to contain the powder is not more than 2 feet square, it may be brought into the chamber ready made; if of greater dimensions, it must be put together on the spot, the pieces to form the sides being arranged in a manner similar to the cases of branches.

One opening is to be left at the top about 4

inches square, for the introduction of the charge, and another in the centre of the side through which to introduce the hose-trough.

The dimensions of the space to contain any given charge are calculated on the supposition that a cubic foot will contain 58·5626 lbs. of powder; 1000 cubic inches will therefore contain 33·89 lbs: and 1 lb. of powder will occupy about 30 cubic inches: therefore, if P represent the given number of pounds of powder, and x be the side of the cube, sought in inches;

$$x = \sqrt[3]{30\,P}.$$

Some miners have imagined that if a vacuum were left about the charge, proportioned to its quantity, its effect would be sensibly increased.

This property of the vacuum is not yet sufficiently proved to allow of its adoption in practice.

It is probable that the addition of a proportion of explosive cotton would add much to the effect of a charge. If the cotton were first introduced, and laid without pressure, but yet compactly enough to sustain the powder, the latter when ignited (say at one third of its depth), would expand, pressing down the cotton, giving time for all the powder to be inflamed, and finally firing a yet more energetic agent.

To place the Hose-Troughs.

217. The hose-troughs are small wooden pipes or tubes in which the powder-hose intended to convey the fire to the charge is placed.

These troughs are made $1\frac{1}{2}$ inches square in the clear. The four pieces of which they are composed are called the sill, sides, and top, or cover: they are all from $\frac{1}{4}$ to $\frac{1}{2}$ an inch in thickness.

The trough should penetrate the powder-case about 4 inches, and should exactly fit the opening left for it, which must be made water-tight.

It is fixed on the floor of the branch by small pickets, to the top of which the sill of the trough is nailed. Sometimes pickets are driven against the sides of the trough to prevent its being disturbed.

The different lengths of the trough should be sawn square off at each end, so that they may fit exactly. Each portion of the trough should always be accompanied by its cover, well fitted, but fastened with one peg only, in order that it may easily be removed to introduce the powder-hose.

The trough makes an elbow when it changes its direction. The pieces forming an elbow should be solidly yet simply connected. Figs.

121 and 122 show the most common forms of elbows.

When several mines are to be fired at the same time, it is necessary to proportion their trains, that is, so to regulate the hose-troughs that, starting from the same point, the distances from that point to the charges may be all equal. To arrive at this result without long trials, proceed as follows:—

For two charges, Fig. 123, place a trough on the shortest line from one to the other, mark the centre of it, and let the principal trough join at that point.

For three charges, Fig. 124, connect, as above, the two which are nearest together. Join the middle point of the first trough to the third charge, and divide into two equal parts the whole length between this third charge and one of the former; then let the principal trough be joined to this last central point.

For four charges, Fig. 125, first connect them two and two, then join the central points, and proceed as above.

The elbows of a trough impede the communication of the fire, for which an allowance must be made when proportioning the trains, each elbow being valued at 3 inches; thus, if on one side of the principal trough there be one elbow more than on the other, the principal trough should be placed 3 inches nearer to that side, which is done by placing it 1½ inches from the central point towards that side.

Square elbows impede the communication of the fire a little more than oblique ones. Experience has also shewn that two powder-hoses may be placed within 18 inches of one another, if covered with earth, and produce separate explosions.

Common Mines.

218. The *line of least resistance* of a mine is a line drawn from the centre of the charge to the point where the charge, when exploded, meets with the least resistance. In common cases, this line is a perpendicular drawn from the centre of the charge to the surface of the ground.

The opening produced by the explosion of a mine is called the crater; its radius at the surface of the ground is called the radius of the crater; and a line drawn from the centre of the charge to any point of the upper edge of the crater, is called the radius of explosion. Thus AB, Fig. 126, is the line of least resistance, BC the radius of the crater, and AC the radius of explosion.

The distance at which a charge can destroy a gallery in its neighbourhood is called the radius of rupture. This radius varies in length according to the direction in which it is measured.

When the radius of rupture is inclined below a horizontal line passing through the charge, it is called the sub-horizontal radius.

Charges which produce a crater the radius of which is equal to the line of least resistance were for a long time the only ones used by miners, and are still called *common mines*.

The form of the solid of earth raised by the explosion of a common mine cannot be exactly known. It is usual to regard it as a frustrum of a cone, having for its height the line of least resistance; for the radius of its larger end, the same line; and for the radius of its smaller end, the half of that line. In this cass, the volume of the common crater will be $1\tfrac{1}{6} l^3$,* or $1\cdot 83\ l^3$, where l represents the line of least resistance.

Miners have held different opinions as to the bulk of the solid removed by the explosion of a common mine. Vauban conceived it to be a perfect cone, whose summit was placed in the centre of the charge, and found for its content $1\cdot 05\ l^3$.

Mesgrigny adopted the truncated cone. Lefebre admits the cone of Vauban, but added $\tfrac{1}{7}$ to it which gives $1\cdot 20\ l^3$.

Vallière imagined it to be a paraboloid, having for its focus the centre of the charge, and found its content $1\cdot 90.\ l^3$. Muller truncated the same

* *Vide* Note II. Appendix.

paraboloid by a plane passing through its focus perpendicular to the line of least resistance, and found its volume 1·84 l^3.

These different ideas as to the forms of craters caused miners to assume very unequal charges of powder as necessary to remove the same mass of earth.

It has been ascertained by experiment that in common mines the horizontal radius of rupture is equal to $1\frac{3}{4}$ times the line of least resistance, or $\frac{7}{4}$ l. In a vertical direction, this radius is of the same length as the radius of explosion, and is consequently represented by $l \sqrt{2}$. For the sub-horizontal directions it is admitted that the extremities of the radii of rupture are situated on the surface of an ellipsoid, having for its semi-axes the horizontal and vertical radii above determined. Any gallery situated within the limits of this ellipsoid will probably be destroyed.*

Independent of the rupture, the explosion of a mine produces a subterraneous commotion capable of destroying or deranging some parts of a gallery without consequently interrupting the communication. Nothing positive can be said as to the distance to which this commotion may extend; and it may even be observed that what has been already stated regarding the radii of rupture is known but in an uncertain manner,

* *Vide* Note III. Appendix.

and that fresh experiments are much required to obtain more perfect information.

219. To find the charge of a common mine in ordinary earth. Express in feet the line of least resistance, and take $\frac{1}{10}$ of its cube for the charge in pounds.

This practical rule is founded on the supposition that the charges are in proportion to the volumes of the craters, and that for similar craters, as all those of common mines are, the charges should be in proportion to the cubes of the lines, of least resistance.

The charge for a common mine may also be found when it is known what quantity of powder is required to raise a cubic yard, by the following rule :—

To find the content of the crater. Take $\frac{1}{6}$ of the cube of the line of least resistance, then multiply this quantity reduced to cubic yards by the quantity of powder required to raise 1 cubic yard for the charge required.

On the Charges of Common Mines, Overcharged Mines, and Undercharged Mines.

220. It has been stated that to find the charge of a common mine in lbs. $\frac{1}{10}$ of the cube of the line of least resistance in feet is to be taken.

This rule, however, is only approximative, and

answers but for one description of earth, namely No. 3 in the following table.

The true rule is founded on the fact, ascertained by experiment, that it requires 1 lb. 5¼ oz., of powder to raise 1 cubic yard of earth similar to No. 3 in the table. Let it be required to find the charge for a common mine under a line of least resistance of 10 feet. The content of the crater is $\frac{1}{6}$ $10^3 = 1833 \cdot 3$ cubic feet $= 67 \cdot 8$ yards and $67 \cdot 8 \times 1$ lb. 5¼ oz., gives about 90 lbs. for the charge, which, according to the rule would be

$$\frac{10^3}{10} = \frac{1000}{10} = 100 \text{ lbs.}$$

thus keeping on the safe side.

To find the charge of a common mine for any other description of earth, rock, or masonry, first find the charge as if it were for No. 3. Then ascertain by weighing one cubic foot of the given substance, to which of the descriptions of earth, rock, or masonry, it belongs, and multiply the charge previously found by the corresponding number in the last column of the table; or find the content of the crater in cubic yards, and multiply it by the charge in the column of charges corresponding to the description of earth, &c., in which the mine is to be placed.

Number.	Description of Earth, Rock, or Masonry.	Weight in lbs. of one cubic foot.	Charges for a cubic yard.	Proportional value of charges.
			lbs. oz	
1	Light sandy earth	84	1 13	1·12
2	Hard sand........................	110	2 0	1·25
3	Fat earth, mixed with sand and gravel, called *common earth*	116	1 10	1·00
4	Wet sand	117	2 2	1·30
5	Earth mixed with small stones	118	2 4	1·40
6	Clay mixed with loam............	124	2 8	1·55
7	Fat earth mixed with pebbles...	142	2 12	1·70
8	Rock	142	3 10	2·25
9	New or old moist masonry or brick-work		2 2	1·30
10	Inferior brick-work or masonry		2 11	1·66
11	Good new brick-work or masonry		3 10	2·25
12	Good old ditto		4 1	2·50
13	Roman ditto, or other equally solid ; good old brick-work or masonry in warm climates		4 11	2·90

221. To find the charge for a "globe of compression," or overcharged mine. If the line of least resistance and the radius of the crater be given, subtract the former from the latter, multiply the remainder by ·8 * to this product add the given line of least resistance, for the line of least resistance of a common mine requiring the same charge as the globe of compression. Then the charge will be equal to $\frac{1}{10}$th of the cube of this line.

The effects of an overcharged mine are deter-

* See Note IV. Appendix.

mined in the same manner as those of a common mine, observing only to use the line of least resistance found for determining the charge, or deduced from the charge, as the case may be, instead of the given line of least resistance.

222. When it is required to determine the charge of an undercharged mine, the same rule may be followed; in this case, however, the quantity produced by multiplying the difference between the line given of least resistance, and the radius of the crater, by ·8, is to be subtracted from the line of least resistance, instead of being added to it as in the former case.

The radius of the crater of an undercharged mine should never be less than $\frac{2}{3}$ of the line of least resistance, otherwise no sensible crater would be produced.

Tamping of Mines.

223. When a charge is lodged at the end of a gallery, the gallery must be filled up, or tamped, to a distance equal to twice the length of the line of least resistance of the mine, measured in a right line from the charge to the end of the tamping.

The proportion in which a charge for a mine is to be increased on account of imperfect tamping, or of its entire suppression, must depend on the size of the gallery or shaft as compared with that of the charge. A very large charge for a globe of compression, at the end of a small gallery, would not probably have its effects perceptibly reduced by omitting the tamping altogether, while, with a very small charge, the expansive force of the explosion would find vent in a large gallery, without producing any material effect.

When it is not required to preserve a small gallery, or a mine is to be sprung at the bottom of a shaft, sunk for the purpose of demolition, and for tamping which time cannot be allowed, the charge must be increased to make up for the diminution or total suppression of the tamping in the following proportions:—

An increase of $\frac{1}{4}$ of the charge is equivalent to a reduction of $\frac{1}{3}$ of the tamping.

An increase of $\frac{1}{3}$ to $\frac{2}{3}$ of the tamping.

It may, therefore, be concluded, that if the charge be doubled the tamping may be wholly dispensed with.

Manner of Firing Mines.

224. There are various methods of firing mines; among these are the *monk*, and the *box-trap.**

These two methods require the use of a powder-hose, by which is meant a long linen bag, from half an inch to an inch in diameter, filled with powder.

* La Bôite de Boule. *Fr.*

The linen used for making the hose should be of a close texture, and the sewing be executed with care.

The monk. Stretch the extremity of the hose upon a sheet of paper, and sprinkle some dry fine powder on it; cover this powder over with another sheet of paper, secured at its four corners with dry earth or stones; pass a pyramid of agarick * through a hole in the upper sheet; its base should be plunged into the powder, and the top be above the upper paper; set fire to the summit of the pyramid with another piece of agarick, usually made in the same form as the first, and retire.

The piece of agarick used to communicate the fire to the powder is called the monk; it should be about $1\frac{1}{2}$ inches long, and be divided by the sheet of paper in two equal parts.

The box-trap, Fig. 132, is 18 inches high, and 6 inches wide in the clear. The bottom consists of a piece of plank 18 by 10 inches, and its cover is fixed at one side only with a wooden pin, about which it can be turned.

At 6 inches from the top of the box a horizontal slit is made in three of its sides, serving to admit a piece of board, which ought to slide freely in it. In the lower part of the box an opening is

* Amadou.

left to admit the powder-hose on the side not cut for the slide.

Place the box against the extremity of the tamping, and secure it well; tie a string to the slide, and lead it along the stanchions of the gallery on pegs introduced for that purpose; put the end of the hose into the box through the hole left for it, and spread on the top of it some fine dry powder; then put in the slide, and close with earth, or rags of sand-bags, all communication between the lower part of the box and the branch; place a star-match of six or eight points, well lighted, on the slide; close the top partly only, then pull the string, and the star will fire the mine.

The two methods above described have the inconvenience of requiring a powder-hose, which, from its own explosion, poisons the galleries. They have also and particularly the monk, the defect of not producing the explosion always at the instant desired

Bickford's Fuze burns more regularly, and is now in general use instead of the hose; it consists of a small flexible waterproof tube containing gunpowder, which will even burn under water.

The Rocket (Fig. 133).

225. This rocket is a common one, terminated with a circular head of wood. To use it, a

wooden trough, with a smooth interior, must extend from the charge to the point where the rocket is to start; tin tubes have been recommended, but are found not to answer. A rocket is then placed in the end of the trough, the quick match with which it is provided is lighted, and the rocket starts with very great velocity, penetrates the charge, and fires it.

When the rocket has to pass elbows, or when it is desired to fire several mines at the same moment, at each turn of the trough a fresh rocket is placed, with its quick-match secured round a nail: the first rocket arriving at the point where the second is placed, fires it. In order the better to insure the first rocket firing the second, a quantity of powder ($\frac{1}{4}$ ounce) should be strewed about the match of the latter, protected by a triangular slip of deal, nailed to the bottom of the trough; the rocket then passes over the powder, which its rapid motion would otherwise disperse.

A rocket may be made to turn in a curved trough, when the radius of that part is not less than twice the length of the rocket.

In order to prevent the smoke of the charge penetrating the gallery through the trough, one or two small iron traps may be placed in the trough, which, being raised by the rocket, fall again by their own weight, and cut off all communication between the gallery and the charge.

The rocket is 6 inches long, will travel 100 yards at least, and its velocity is so great, that two rockets fired at the same moment, to run very different distances, leave no perceptible interval in the times of their arrival. This property renders it easy to proportion the tubes of mines to be fired simultaneously, which, with powder-hose, requires great nicety.

The common rocket contains $\frac{3}{4}$ of an ounce of a composition formed $\frac{2}{5}$ of fine powder, $\frac{2}{5}$ salt-petre, and $\frac{1}{5}$ of charcoal-dust. These ingredients should be very carefully mixed, otherwise some portions of it might explode. Its diameter is nearly $\frac{3}{4}$ of an inch, and its entire weight is about $1\frac{1}{2}$ ounce. They may be made much smaller when required.

Firing Mines by Voltaic Electricity.

226. In many cases the use of a Voltaic Battery to fire mines will be found of great advantage. This mode of exploding charges (even when under water) was first suggested by the author of this volume,* and has been very successfully applied in many well-known cases of sub-marine explosions. The peculiar advantages it offers are, that the effect is instantaneous and certain, if only ordinary care has been taken in the preliminary arrangements; that when acids or salt are

* See Note 5

not present, no precautions are necessary to preserve the wires (which serve instead of powder-hose) from damp; that if the wires are introduced through a carefully closed orifice, in a well-soldered tin or iron case, the charge may be placed in the required position long before it is wanted, which may be frequently useful in defensive mining operations; that many charges may be simultaneously exploded, or they may be exploded in any series of succession required, without any complex arrangements. The only precautions required to insure all these desirable results being, to take care that a sufficiently powerful battery is provided—that the copper wire is of proper size—that no more platinum or iron wire is used for firing the charges than the battery is capable of rendering red hot at the distance of the greatest charge, or at the distance of one-half the length of all the wire used—and that the wires do not touch any other conducting body, or each other. It would be well, therefore, to have the copper wire coated with some non-conducting varnish, as india rubber disolved in naptha, or sealing-wax varnish.

In submarine explosions, the wires, being coated with a water-proof composition, should be secured on opposite sides of a rope, first passed slowly through boiling Stockholm tar; the whole may then be served with spun yarn, and at the same time well coated with a mixture composed of one pound of pitch, two ounces of tallow, and two ounces of bees' wax, melted and well mixed (but not boiled) and applied hot. In the explosion of very large charges it would be well to have three or four sets of wires to fire the charge in as many differents points at the same instant, which would necessarily secure the ignition of a large proportion of the charge, and produce so much greater effect. There can be no difficulty in putting three, four, or more sets of wires to one rope; it will only be necessary to coat them well with the mixture above mentioned, serving each wire at the same time with cotton tape well saturated with the same mixture. Of course when several sets of wires are used a corresponding power of batteries must be provided; and great care must be taken that all the wires are brought into contact with the poles of the battery at the same instant. Each end of a very stout copper wire may be connected with four smaller copper wires within the chamber, the volume of the latter wires being equal to that of the larger. Before firing any very large charge, an experiment might easily be made to ascertain whether the batteries are of sufficient power for the purpose designed or not; the more especially as such an experiment would take but little time, be made at very trifling cost, and assure the engineer of the certainty of success. Stout annealed copper wire must be used as the conducting agent, and very fine platinum wire to fire the charge; but when platinum wire cannot be obtained, very fine iron wire, or a fine needle, or a nail beat or drawn out to a fine thread, may be used; in these latter cases, however, it would add much to the certainty of the operation, if a small quantity of explosive cotton were loosely wrapped round part of the iron wire, or needle; for as the cotton will explode at a temperature greatly below red heat, the explosion might be effected with much less voltaic power than would otherwise be necessary.

Blasts.

227. Blasts are small chambers or holes made in rock or masonry whenever the ordinary method of excavation becomes too tedious. The excavation of blast-holes requires the use of particular tools, called borers, jumpers, scrapers, needles, and tamping bars.

To form the blast-hole, two or three men are required; one holds the borer with both hands, while one or two others strike the head of it with sledge hammers. The first turns the borer in every direction, so that the hole may be circular, and from time to time clears it out with the scraper.

When the hole is not required to exceed 15 inches in depth, the whole may be excavated in the above manner; but if required to be 20 inches, or more, deep, the jumper is made use of. The miner holds the jumper in both hands, raises it, and lets it fall in the hole, turning it continually; he also clears the hole with the scraper. When the stone is of a very hard description, it is usual to pour water occasionally into the jumper-hole.

To load the hole, fill about one-fourth or one-third of it with powder, according to the nature of the stone. The charge for a depth of 18 inches is from 8 to 12 ounces.

To tamp and prime the blast-hole, the needle is first introduced, plunging it well into the powder, and placing it on the smoothest side of the hole; then a layer of clay is laid on the powder, and is closely pressed down with the tamping bar.

Other similar layers are then laid, or layers of brick reduced to small bits, the needle being turned repeatedly. It is usual to press down the first layers with a bar of wood, the helve of a tool, for instance; and the latter ones with the iron tamping bar. When the hole is thus filled up, a small shell of clay is formed round the needle, which is then withdrawn, the hole left by it is filled with fine powder, and it is fired with a "monk" or a piece of port-fire.

The use of the needle is often dispensed with,

in which case the priming is rolled up in a sheet of brown paper, or it is introduced in straw-stalks thrust into one another. This priming is placed in the hole at the same time as the charge, so that it may penetrate well into the latter.* The tamping is then executed as before.

The use of the tamping bar may also be dispensed with, filling the whole with very fine dry sand, without any pressure.

Three miners can bore and charge in a day three holes each, 21 inches deep. If they have very good tools, they can perform the above work in four hours and a half.

When the blast has been fired, the pieces of stone are removed with the aid of crow-bars, and the proper form is given to the excavation.

The result of many experiments has shewn that in blasting rock a large portion of the powder (nearly half) may be dispensed with, by mixing with the remaining powder fine dry sawdust of elm or beech. A blast thus prepared will have as great an effect as if powder alone were used; the pieces of rock detached are, however, larger, and to subdivide them, a frequent use of the sledge hammer is required.†

---

* Bickford's "fuze" has now superseded the use of either needle or port-fire, and it is perfectly safe. It has been tried at Chatham, and found to answer well.

† See a Memoir of M. Leblanc in No. VII. of the Memorial de l'Off. du Génie.

Demolitions.

228. The charges of mines intended to overturn masonry are calculated as if they were to be exploded in common soil, but increased in the proportions shewn in the table for the different kinds of masonry to be destroyed.

To Breach a Wall standing alone.

First ascertain as nearly as possible the thickness of the wall, and then proceed thus :—

First case.—When the wall is from 2 to 3 feet thick, place one or two barrels of powder against the lower part of it, and fire them.

Second case.—When the wall is from 5 to $6\frac{1}{2}$ feet thick, place one or two charges under its foundations beneath the centre of the wall.

Third case.—When the wall is from 9 to 12 feet thick, open at the foot of it, or about 1 foot above the water level, a branch gallery, which must be driven to the centre of the wall; then make two returns perpendicular to this branch, and place the powder in their extremities, Fig. 134.

To Breach a Wall supporting a Terrace.

Open at the foot of the wall, or one foot above the level of the water, a branch perpendicular to the direction of the revetment; drive it through the wall to the earth, then make to the right and left two other branches, along the back of the wall, and equal to its thickness in length; place the charges at the ends of these branches, so that the centre of the charge may be flush with the back of the wall.

Demolition of Revetments.

229. When the revetment is without counterforts, or the counterforts are not more than 3 feet thick, several branches are driven perpendicular to the direction of the revetment, at equal distances apart. The charges used should produce craters that would cross each other a little.

When the wall has counterforts of the common dimensions, the charges are placed as far as practicable, in the centre of them, at their junction with the revetment, Fig. 135.

When but little time is allowed, instead of making one opening for a pair of charges, one is made for each, and they are placed at three-fourths of the thickness of the wall, and so regulated that their craters may slightly cross one another, Fig. 136.

When galleries cannot be driven at the proper level for the charge, as in the demolition of wharfs, &c., shafts are sunk behind the revetment, or at a short distance in the rear of it, Fig. 137, and branches are then driven to the positions for the charges; or, which is still better, because it is a more speedy operation a shaft may be sunk for each charge.

The depth of the shafts must be sufficient to admit of a proper length of tamping.

If at the same time with the wall a mass of earth in rear of it is to be brought down, prolong the branches into the interior of the mass sufficiently to allow of the mines at the back of the wall exploding before those placed at their extremities, Fig. 138.

When there is a gallery, Fig. 139, at the back of the revetment, the charges should be placed in this gallery, excavating chambers for them in the revetment at distances apart equal to twice their line of least resistance, viz., at two lined intervals.

All the gallery occupied by the charges is then tamped; the length of the tamping at each end should be equal to twice the line of least resistance of the extreme charges.

The following method is employed also with success. Regarding as the line of least resistance the distance from the gallery to the exterior surface of the wall, imagine a row of common mines placed at two-lined intervals throughout the length, calculate the sum of their charges, to which add one-half for a great gallery; place the whole charge in several heaps, with strong trains leading from one to another. Then tamp strongly and carefully the ends of the gallery, leaving the space intended to be demolished, void. When the gallery is more than 2 yards wide and high, or if it have many issues difficult to tamp, the charge of powder must be proportionably augmented.

Demolition of a Tower.

230. If the interior diameter of the tower be 6 yards or more, Fig. 140, drive galleries into the wall from the interior of the tower, and place charges so as to be a little nearer to the interior than to the exterior surface of the wall. When the tower is connected with walls, charges must be placed at their points of junction.

When the tower is but 4 or 5 yards in diameter Fig. 141, sink a shaft to about the level of the bottom of the foundations, and place a charge there corresponding to the line of least resistance measured from the centre of the charge to the foot of the wall outside.

Cover the floor of the tower with two rows of small beams; then lay two beams crossing and halved into one another, and propped against the masonry of the arch.

When a shaft cannot be sunk on account of water, and when the tower has loop holes which prevent charges being placed in the walls, lay the charge on the floor of the tower enclosed in a strongly constructed case, propped on all sides against the masonry.

When the tower is square, and has several floors or stages, the charges may be placed at the four corners of the ground-story, tamping the first floor.

Demolition of a Powder-Magazine.

231. Place charges in the piers and gable ends, so that their craters may slightly cross each other.

When time presses, a charge is laid on the floor of the magazine, the doors are barricaded, and it is fired with a hose led outside.

To determine the quantity of powder required for the heap, calculate the number of common mines required to overturn a revetment of the same length and thickness as the walls of the magazines, including the piers; add one half to the sum of the charges thus found, and place the whole in one heap in the centre of the magazine.

The above method is only applicable to magazines of not more than 150 square yards surface. If of greater capacity, the quantity first found should be increased $\frac{1}{10}$ for every 15 square yards of additional surface, and be placed in two or more heaps connected with powder-hose, to fire them simultaneously.

Demolition of Bridges.

232. To destroy a bridge the piers of which are from 4 feet 3 inches to 5 feet 2 inches thick, place in one of the piers two charges of 130 to 160 lbs. each, Fig. 142, and secure a plank to the bridge, on which to place the powder-hose.

If the pier be from $6\frac{1}{2}$ to 10 feet thick, drive in the middle of it parallel to its side, two small branches, at the ends of which place charges of from 200 to 230 lbs. each, Fig. 143.

When there is not time to place charges in the interior of the piers, cut a trench over the key of the arch 18 inches deep, in which place 400 to 530 lbs. of powder.

This quantity of powder has broken semi-circular arches of 26 ft. span, and $4\frac{1}{4}$ ft. thickness at the crown.

A trench in the form of a cross. Fig. 143, may be excavated over the middle of the arch, each branch 10 feet long, and carried down to the upper surface of the arch. Place in each branch 200 lbs. of powder for an arch $3\frac{1}{4}$ feet thick, and cover the charges with timber, earth, &c.

An arch may also be blown up by suspending an open trough under it with cords, and placing in it charges of powder similar to those already stated for trenches cut on the surface.

When the saving of powder is of consequence,

sink a shaft down to one of the haunches, Fig. 144, and place the powder in one mass, unless the bridge be very wide: an arch of 18 inches, or 2 feet in thickness, of a bridge 20 feet wide, may thus be destroyed with 45 lbs. of powder, if a loading can be applied over the charge giving an equal resistance throughout.

If the bridge be more than 20 feet wide, two shafts must be sunk, and charged as before described. When the side walls of the bridge above the piers are slightly built, and the loading of the arch is of loose rubbish, a small gallery should be driven about 5 or 6 feet from the arch stones, to the centre of the bridge, as at A, Fig. 144; a return is then made towards the arch, and the charge is placed in contact with it. Bridges of timber may be blown up by suspending barrels of powder underneath.

Demolition of a House.

233. Begin by undermining the windows and doors, and cuttting away the piers between them, so as to leave the building supported by a few piers only, nearly square. Place then in each of these piers, a charge of from 13 to 16 lbs. of powder, tamping well with wood. Proportion the trains to the different charges, so that they may be simultaneously exploded.

234. To destroy palisades, or gates, doors, &c.,

the best method is to suspend a leathern bag filled with powder, either with a forked stick, strong gimlet, or stout nail, against the gate or palisade. The bag should have about an inch of port-fire firmly secured in one side of it, to communicate the fire to the charge. To throw down a strong palisade, from 30 to 50 lbs. of powder should be used. To burst open a town gate, 60 or 70 lbs. of powder will be required.

Of Fougasses.

235. *Of Common Fougasses.*—Mines are so called when placed at the bottoms of small shafts from 9 to 12 feet deep. The powder is lodged in one of the sides of the shaft, and it is fired from a secure spot by means of a powder-hose brought up one side of the shaft, and carried in a trough parallel to the ground 5 or 6 feet below the surface. When there is no reason to fear shells, it will be sufficient to keep the trough 2 or $2\frac{1}{2}$ feet under the ground. The powder-case and trough should be well pitched, the shaft tamped in the strongest manner, and the earth round about the shaft be dug over, that nothing may indicate to the enemy the position of the fougasse.

Of Shell Fougasses.

236. Shells may be buried singly, or in small heaps, and be made to burst either under the ground, or on its surface.

If they are to burst underground, they must be sufficiently charged to produce a crater, through which the pieces are projected.

If they are to burst on the surface, the requisite quantity of powder to produce a crater and throw out the shells must be lodged under them, while these latter need only have a sufficient charge to burst them.

In all cases a box is used, Fig. 145, divided into two parts by a partition. The shells are placed in the upper part, their fuzes project through the partition, and extend from ½ to 1 inch below it.

In the lower part the hose only is placed when the shells are intended to produce their own crater, but power sufficient to produce the crater is introduced when they are intended to burst on the surface of the ground.

Description of shell.	Full charge of the shell.		Depth at which the full charge produces a crater.	
	lb.	oz.	′	″
Calibre, 5½	1	0	2	0
,, 8	2	9	2	10
,, 10	5	0	3	6
,, 13	11	0	4	7

Common and shell fougasses produce an effect only near to their craters, consequently they should be exploded at the moment when the enemy is above them.

Of Stone Fougasses.

237. Stone fougasses offer the advantage over those already described of extending their effects to a great distance; and as they can be easily and speedily executed, they are applicable in field fortification to the defence of ditches and of salient angles; and in permanent fortifications, to the defence of flèches, and other advanced works, and particularly to the defence of breaches.

The most simple method of forming a stone fougasse is to excavate an inclined cavity, as represented in Fig. 146, of from 5 to 6 feet deep. At the bottom a box is to be placed, containing 55 lbs. of powder; from this box a powder-hose is led to the point at which it is intended to fire the fougasse, or it may be fired by a rocket, art. 226.

A strong shield of wood is placed in front of the charge perpendicular to the axis of the fougasse; 3 or 4 cubic yards of pebbles, or an equal weight of other materials, are then filled in over the shield; the earth above the pebbles is to be retained by a revetment of sod-work, or boards, and well rammed. A sufficient body of earth must be helped above the charge to insure its taking effect in the direction required. A fougasse of this kind may be prepared beforehand, and loaded from the rear through a wooden trough introduced for that purpose, which is then tamped with sand-bags filled with earth, each sand-bag being rammed down with a beam.

Twelve men can make a stone fougasse 6 feet deep in three hours; which, being charged as before described, will, when exploded, disperse the materials over a space 60 yards in length and 50 yards in width.

CHAPTER XI.

ON THE ATTACK OF FORTRESSES.

238. The first operation of a besieging army is to *invest* the fortress intended to be attacked. The number and description of troops required for this service must depend upon the strength of the opposing garrison, and the nature of the surrounding ground. If the fortress be situated in a level open country, then the greater part of the investing corps should be composed of cavalry; if in a broken or mountainous tract, then bodies of light infantry are preferable; but whatever the site of the fortress may be, the investing corps should generally contain three or four regiments of light dragoons, with a proportion of field-artillery.

The march of this corps should be so regulated that every avenue to the place may be occupied at the same time. During the day, the troops are to be kept out of the range of the enemy's guns, but towards the evening strong parties should gradually be pushed forward, to shut in the garrison as closely as possible. The objects of this first operation, which is called the *Investment*, are to secure all the cattle and forage in the vicinity;

to prevent any person escaping from the fortress, or any succours, either of troops, provisions, or ammunition, being thrown into it; and to support the reconnoissance made by the engineers, who, during the investment, are employed in taking notes of the description of the different fronts, and correcting their plan of the fortress, or making one.

This plan should be on a sufficiently large scale to show clearly the nature of the ground within 3000 yards of the most advanced works of the place, viz. the course of rivers or streams, ravines, and roads; the extent of inundations, marshes, and woods; and, in short, everything which might tend to the advantage of the attack, or the contrary. The reconnoissance should be made on every front, in order to keep the enemy in ignorance as to the front or fronts intended to be attacked.

Although in ordinary cases, as explained in art. 44, lines of contravallation may be dispensed with, yet if the garrison of the place attacked be numerous and well organized, it is advisable to construct forts or redoubts to command the approaches to the camps, and the flanks of the attack.

239. During the period of the investment the engineers not only correct their plan of the place, from their own observations, but they should also

endeavour to discover on what fronts working parties have recently been employed; whether any galleries have been driven under the glacis or elsewhere; in what parts the principal magazines, barracks, and stores are situated; the positions of the principal squares, and place of exercise for the troops; what number of regiments there are in the garrison; whether they were often manœuvred in the outskirts of the town; what number of cavalry are in the fortress, &c., &c. They then mark accurately with pickets on the ground the prolongations of all the faces of the most salient works, and also of their capitals; the former prolongations should be those of the crests of the parapets, and must be determined with the utmost accuracy; for as the first batteries thrown up are placed on the prolongation of these lines, it follows that they must of necessity be included within the limits of the first parallel, Fig. 163. The positions of the several pickets marking these prolongations should be accurately laid down on the plan: the best times for observing the prolongations of the faces of a work are at the rising and setting of the sun.

240. The alignement of the capitals is required, because it is across these lines that the besieger makes his approaches towards the place; and he does so for the following reasons;—

1st. That they mark the shortest road towards the

salient angles, where he must of necessity first arrive, those being the points to which he is nearest.

2ndly. That he is there less exposed to the enemy's fire, since he cannot be seen by the work nearest to him, and towards which he is approaching; and,

3dly. That his approaches being kept near the capitals, they do not, in general, mask the fire of his own enfilading batteries.

The prolongation of the capitals need not, however, be so strictly ascertained as those of the crests of the parapets, because it is of no consequence whether the approaches extend equally to the right and left of them, or not.

Besides the operations already detailed, during the period of the investment, working parties are employed in the neighbouring woods, making gabions, fascines, mining-frames, and gallery-cases; preparing platforms, timber for magazines, and, if necessary, clearing roads for the transport of the battering train to the great park of artillery.

241. These preliminary arrangements being made, let us examine what is the object of the assailant, and how he may best proceed to effect it. His object is to possess himself of a fortress which impedes his progress, or cramps his operations; and he having usually eight or ten times

as many troops as are supposed to be shut up in the fortress, it follows that the greater number will overpower the less, so soon as they are brought to contend hand to hand.

But the field of battle of the garrison is so organized as to prevent this collision, being surrounded with obstacles which the besieger must overturn, before he can reap the advantage of his numerical superiority.

To reduce as much as possible the necessary sacrifices of a besieger, he is compelled to make his attack in a systematic manner, requiring more or less time in proportion to the strength of the place attacked, and the valour of its garrison.

The mode of attack resorted to since the invention of artillery, consists—

1st. In assailing only one or two fronts.

2ndly. In destroying the fire of those fronts.

3dly. In making roads by which the assailant may advance unseen to the foot of the ramparts; and,

4thly. In opening those ramparts, forming practicable breaches therein.

When these works are executed in such a manner as to prevent the besieged obstructing the passage of his foe from the camp to the foot of the breach, the adversaries are then placed so nearly on an equality, that the small garrison must eventually be overpowered by the more numerous troops of the besieger.

The most speedy mode in which any number of men can make for themselves a road, in which they would be concealed from the view of an enemy, is—first to trace the road, so that, if produced, its prolongations would pass clear of the most salient points occupied by him within the range of artillery—and then to dig a trench in that direction, throwing the earth excavated towards the enemy, and making the bottom of that trench of sufficient width to serve as the road required.

242. The project of attack being determined on, the fire of the fronts attacked is to be destroyed. Now it has been ascertained by experiment, that at 400 yards distant, two-thirds of the shot fired from heavy ordnance will take effect; at 600 yards, two fifths to three-fifths; at 800 yards, not more than two-fifths: whence we may assume that the first batteries thrown up in a siege ought not to be much more than 600 yards from the works intended to be enfiladed by them, because at a greater distance three-fifths of the ammunition would be uselessly expended.

The best offensive position that the besieger can take up is to open a continuous trench as near the place as is safe, and parallel to the general contour of the works, whence it is called the *first parallel, or place of arms* (Fig. 163), its use being to serve as a communication between the several batteries first thrown up, and also as a place of arms, in which to post the guard of the trenches or troops supporting the attack, who, during the night on which this work is commenced, take post about 100 yards in front of the parallel. The extremities or wings of this parallel are sometimes strengthened with redoubts, and, in general, epaulments to cover cavalry are thrown up a little in rear of those wings or redoubts.

It is desirable to trace the first parallel within less than 600 yards of the place, if its defective situation, insufficient or inexpert garrison, or other favourable circumstances, will permit.

To communicate between the first parallel and the camp, zig-zag roads (Fig. 163) are formed crossing the capitals, and so directed that their prolongations may pass in front of the most salient works of the enemy situated within the range of heavy artillery.

243. The opening of the first parallel, and the zig-zag communications in rear of it, is called the *opening of the trenches*, and this work is usually completed in the first period of twenty-four hours.

Under the protection of the first parallel, batteries of guns, howitzers, and mortars, are constructed to destroy the fire of the works attacked;

and zig-zag roads are excavated in front of the parallel, crossing the capitals as before, and defiladed from the enemy's works; under cover of their parapets, the assailant advances to within about 300 yards of the salient angles of the fortress, where he forms a *second parallel*, (Fig. 163), or place of arms. This is necessary, because he must always have a place of arms nearer the head of his attack than those possessed by the enemy, in order to give it support.

In front of, or in the second parallel, batteries are again constructed, to enfilade the faces and flanks of the works attacked; or to counter-batter any collateral works of the enemy, the prolongations of which either have not been, or could not be embraced by the first parallel, though their fire must be subdued.

244. From the second parallel the assailant again advances in zig-zags towards the place; and when arrived at about 150 yards from the enemy's covered way, he forms other places of arms, called *demi-parallels*, their object being to support the head of the attack, and to procure a position for the more advantageous use of small mortars, which at this period of the siege, are required to drive the infantry out of the salient angles of the covered way.

The besieger then continues to advance, as before, until he arrives at the foot of the glacis, where he forms a *third parallel*.

245. The next operation of the besieger is to *crown the covered way*, and this may be done either by assault or by the continuation of the approaches. The former method has been frequently tried, and has often failed.

When it is intended to crown the covered way by assault, the interior of the third parallel is formed in steps, Fig. 115, on both sides of the capital of the works to be assaulted, in order that the storming and working parties may show a large front. The storming party rush boldly into the covered way, and force the enemy into the places of arms, occupying the traverses of the covered way, behind which they procure such shelter as their delapidated state may afford. The working party in the meanwhile, place their gabions as speedily as possible, on the lines of the proposed trenches, and lose no time in covering themselves.

These trenches are, in the first instance, not extended further than the second traverse of the covered way, the crowning of which to that distance will be sufficient to ensure its possession to the assailant.

246. If systematic approaches are resorted to, the besieger works on from the third parallel, forming what are called the *circular portions;* these are traced across the capitals, so that each is a segment of a circle, its chord 60 or 80 yards long,

and height 20 or 30 yards. On the reverse of this circular portion are collected the materials for the further progress of the attack, which consists of a double sap, art. 247, Figs. 158 and 159, directed along the capital. Having arrived within 30 or 40 yards of the salient angle of the covered way, the besieger turns to the right and left, forming trenches parallel to its crests, and carried to about 15 or 20 yards beyond their prolongations; a return is then made in the trench, and the whole of the end of each is converted into a *trench cavalier*, Fig. 160; the object of which being to obtain a superiority of position for the infantry, it follows that the crest of the trench cavalier must be raised high enough to command the covered way, the defenders of which are then compelled to retire behind the traverses of the places of arms.

The besieger again advances on the capital, and when at 6 or 7 yards from the salient angle of the covered way, the trench is carried parallel to its branches, so as to leave 15 or 18 feet of earth between it and the interior slope of the glacis. As soon as these works are sufficiently carried forward, the lodgment is converted into batteries, to breach the faces of the bastion through the ditches of the ravelin, to breach the salient angle of the ravelin, and to counterbatter the planks of the collateral bastions; these latter batteries being constructed on the crest of the glacis of the body of the place.

While these several breaching and counterbatteries are being completed, and when completed employed in battering the revetments, a descent is made into the ditch of the ravelin, Fig. 164. A breach being made, the assailant saps from the bottom of the descent, across the ditch of the ravelin, and makes a lodgment on the top of the breach, supported by a fire of musketry; this secures to him the possession of the ravelin, along the ditch of which he pushes a zig-zag sap, towards the breach in the face of the bastion, which, if there be any formidable intrenchment in the interior, must be crowned. This lodgment is then extended along the terreplein of the bastion unoccupied by the intrenchments of the besieged. Portions of it are converted into batteries, to breach the enemy's intrenchments; and this done, the garrison can only continue to resist by occupying the neighbouring houses, which they must have previously fortified in the manner already described. When the houses are built in a solid manner, and are favourably situated for defence, the besiegers may yet find much to do if the exertions of a valorous garrison are directed by the skill of well-instructed officers.

247. Having given this general description of the mode of attack adopted against fortresses, it

remains to be shewn in what manner the various works are to be executed. It is not intended to give any very minute details on this subject, but only such as are necessary to render the above description more easily understood.

The first parallel, and the communications between it and the depôts or camps, are traced on the ground with a cord, having pieces of white tape fastened to it, and dividing it into portions each 6 feet long. The working party, each man carrying a pickaxe and shovel, advance by the most convenient routes which the ground presents in single file. On arriving at the position of the parallel, they form a line and extend, each man occupying one of the spaces 6 feet long—their tasks, for eight hours' work being to excavate that length of trench, making it 5 feet wide, and 3 feet deep. The troops who relieve them, if also working 8 hours, widen the trench 5 feet, and the third relief completes it to the form shewn in Figs. 151 and 152; some portions of the parallel being made with steps (Fig. 153), to facilitate the advance of the guard of the trenches, if required to repel sorties. There should be four reliefs for the working party, and each relief should work 8 hours, or until their task is completed, Sometimes a light fascine is used to mark each task, in which case they are placed end to end, and touching each other, in front of the tracing line.

If the working party be armed, the officer arranging them takes each man's musket as he files up, and places it parallel to, and about 8 feet in the rear of, the parallel; each man has then to excavate the trench in front of his own musket. The arrangements of the working party for throwing up the enfilading and counter batteries, would be similar to those already detailed in art. 68. Sometimes it is necessary, on account of the thinness of the layer of earth, or the small depth to which a ditch can be sunk without coming to water, or from its being necessary to procure cover in the shortest possible time, that men should be employed both in front and rear of the battery throwing up earth to form its parapet.

It has already occurred (and no doubt will again), that the parapet or epaulment has been formed entirely of earth in sand-bags; one of the most extensive parapets ever thrown up in one night was made in the manner just described.*

The zig-zag communications between the first and second parallels are traced and executed in the same manner as the first parallel; but when the head of the attack is within the range of grape shot, it is necessary to procure cover for the workmen with as little delay as possible; and gabions are therefore used to revet the interior of the second parallel. One half of the

* At the siege of Gibraltar.

gabions are placed by one party, and the trench in rear of them is dug by another, who bring the rest of the gabions; or the same working party place all the gabions and excavate the trench, in which case each man carries two gabions, a pickaxe, and a shovel, having always to excavate part of the trench in rear of *two* gabions, 4 feet long. During the night, large portions of the trenches in front of the second parallel may be commenced in the manner just described and be finished during the day; but in the day-time no *advance* can usually be made above ground until the besiegers have silenced the artillery of the fortress. The Engineer must then exercise his peculiar art of sapping, by which he is enabled to continue advancing in the face of the enemy's musketry fire.

Fig. 157 represents a plan and section of the *single sap*, used in the formation of the approaches, parallels, and crowning of the covered way. A *squad* of 1 non-commissioned officer and 4 sappers is required for each, and they should be provided with 5 pickaxes, 4 shovels, 3 sap forks (one long and two short), 1 measuring rod, and 1 mallet. The head of the sap is covered by a sap-roller, which consists of a gabion, 6 feet long and 4 feet in diameter, inside of which another $2\frac{1}{2}$ feet in diameter is fixed, the space between them being filled with pickets, to make it bullet proof, and the side is sometimes protected by a cast-iron or wooden shield or mantlet. The first and second sappers work on their knees. The first excavates a trench 18 inches wide and deep, leaving a berm of 1 foot; the second widens the work of the first 20 inches; the third stands upright and deepens the work of the second 18 inches; and the fourth widens the whole trench 10 inches: 4 additional men, to relieve them, are employed in bringing up materials, and these are ready to provide for casualties. A sap-faggot, Fig. 149, is placed between each pair of gabions, to catch any bullets which might otherwise pass between them. The sap-faggot has a strong stake in the middle, which, being driven into the ground, secures it in its place. Instead of a sap-faggot, two sand-bags filled with earth, placed on end one above the other, are preferred.

When it is necessary to form batteries within musket range of the works occupied by the enemy, portions of the parallels may be converted into sunken batteries, Fig. 162. In this case, a communication must be made round each, in its rear, that the service of the battery may not be disturbed by the passage of bodies of men through it.

The approaches may often require a greater relief than the parallels, because they are obliquely traced with regard to the general contour of the fortress, and consequently their parapets have to cover a greater width of trench than those of the parallels. This additional relief is given by placing two fascines on the gabions, side by side, and one over all, as shewn in Fig. 156: the fascines used are 6 feet long and 9 inches in diameter.

When the angle formed by the adjacent zigzags becomes very small, or rather when 100 yards of the zig-zag does not push the approaches so much as 32 yards in advance (those being the proportionate rates at which the single and double saps can be executed), then they should be direct, and consist of *double saps*, as represented in Figs. 158 and 159. That shewn in Fig. 158 may be made serpentine or zig-zag, for defilade; and that in Fig. 159 is covered by traverses constructed by the squad in the centre, and is pushed on *direct* to the front. It may sometimes be necessary to cover the direct saps in the manner shewn in Fig. 161.

Since the trenches cannot be advanced during daylight while the artillery of the fortress remain unsilenced, it must evidently be one of the first objects of the besieger to destroy that artillery; but when the guns are placed under the protection of good traverses, and in blinded batteries, this will be a very tedious operation, which the besieger may, however, with skill and perseverance be able to effect. When the infantry of the besieger are once placed within easy musket-range of the enemy's guns, the latter will soon be silenced; the heads of the attack should therefore always be manned with good marksmen, as soon as a favourable position for them is obtained. The better to effect this object and to support the sap-heads, portions of parallels, called demi-parallels, are formed, in which small mortars are also placed to enfilade the outworks and branches of the covered way, and to shell the enemy's intrenchments in the places of arms.

248. To estimate the strength of working parties, the number of tools, and the quantity of materials required for each night's work, exclusive of reserves, the following assumptions may be made.

In the execution of the first parallel and its communications, together with the approaches between the first and second parallels, one man, with a pickaxe and shovel, excavates 6 feet lineal of the trench.

To throw up an elevated battery, if revetted with fascines, the following working party, materials, and tools are required:—

For each Gun, Howitzer, Mortar, Traverse, or epaulment.
2 Sappers with 6 Infantry, to revet the work.   12 Infantry to excavate the ditch, and form the parapet.

9 Pickaxes.
15 Shovels.
14 Fascines, 18 feet long each.
1 Field-service level.
1 Six-feet rod.
1 Bundle of matches to every 3 guns, &c.
1 Lantern, ditto.
1 Bundle of 50 pickets to 6 fascines.
3 Mauls.
3 Rammers.
1 Bill-hook.
1 Saw to every 2 guns, &c.
1 Hatchet per gun, &c.
1 lb. of candles, ditto.
1 Bundle of gads to each gun, &c.
1 Tape of 50 feet in length per battery.

249. To throw up an elevated battery, if revetted with gabions:—

For each Gun, Howitzer, Mortar, Traverse, or Epaulment.

2 Sappers, to fix gabions, &c.
12 Infantry.
6 Pickaxes.
12 Shovels.
22 Gabions for each gun or epaulment.
15 Gabions for each mortar.
40 Gabions for each traverse.
2 Fascines for each gun, &c.
50 Sand-bags for each traverse.
3 Rammers for each gun, &c.
1 Maul, ditto.
1 Hatchet, ditto.
1 Field-service level, ditto.
1 Six-feet rod, ditto.
1 Bundle of matches to 3 guns, &c.
1 Lantern, ditto.
1 lb. of candles, ditto.

250. To lay a platform.

3 Sappers.
3 Infantry.
3 Pickaxes.
3 Shovels.
6 Rack-lashings and sticks.

251. For each gun or howitzer platform.

1 Stout fascine 9 feet long, to serve as a hurter.
20 Strong pickets, to secure the sleepers of the platform in their berths.
1 Mallet for driving the pickets.

The sleepers of the mortar platform must be similarly secured.

If the site of a platform required excavation or filling up, that work is supposed to have been done by the last relief employed on the battery.

252. For the formation of each powder magazine:—

2 Sappers.	1 Set of magazine timbers.*
10 Infantry.	1 Large tarpaulin.
10 Pickaxes.	4 Common gallery frames.*
10 Shovels.	50 Pieces of sheeting.*
4 Rammers.	8 Fascines.

253. For the execution of a *flying sap*, which is formed with gabions, one infantry soldier, with a pickaxe and shovel, to 2 gabions, or a length of 4 feet.

The task for each man should be, to make the trench 6 feet wide and 3 feet deep behind the two gabions, leaving a berm of 1½ feet.

254. For the execution of single and double saps:—Three reliefs of four sappers to each single sap, viz., twelve sappers, who should be relieved every four hours at least; two sand-bags or one sap-faggot for each gabion; one sap-roller for each single sap; and four or five sap-rollers for

* The powder-magazines may be made with gabions and fascines, with flooring-joists or stout limbs of trees, or boards on edge, to form the ceiling, placed touching one another, covered with fascines and earth. These materials can generally be procured on the spot, and save the transport of magazine timbers, &c.

each double sap, which requires the same number of men as 3 single saps.

To widen the saps into trenches, infantry are required at the rate of 1 man to 2 yards.

255. To calculate the number of men, &c., required to supply the quantity of fascines and gabions demanded, see art. 74, 75, and 81; to which it is only necessary to add, that for the six-feet fascine, two bill-hooks, one saw, one fascine-choaker, and three fascine-horses, are required; and that thirteen men can make five gabions in three-quarters of an hour, their tools being one saw, two bill-hooks, five mallets, and five directing circles.

Four sappers can make a large sap-roller in six hours.

It is to be understood that the men employed in making fascines and gabions must have been previously taught, otherwise they would be a much longer time making any given number than has been above assumed.

CHAPTER XII.

MILITARY RECONNOISSANCE.

256. When no accurate map of the country which is the seat of war can be obtained, or when the map possessed (as is generally the case) is on too small a scale to show its military features in the requisite detail, the General commanding, or the Chief of his staff, sends out individuals properly qualified to examine and make representations of such portions of it as he intends to occupy, or may be compelled to move his troops upon; and the delineation of these features so obtained is called a Military Sketch, which differs from an ordinary map on a large scale in having only such pretensions to trigonometrical accuracy as the time allowed, and the circumstances under which it may be necessary to make it, leave in the power of the individuals employed to bestow.

Sketches are made either,

1st. Simply for the march of troops from one station to another, without reference to an enemy

2dly. When the ground to be moved on is occupied by an enemy whom it is intended to force.

3rdly. When retreating before an enemy.

4thly. When time and security permit a more accurate delineation of the ground.

It is presumed that the beginner in field-sketching has already learned to copy plans, and can use his pencil and pen freely in describing the slopes of ground.

To acquire a facility in using his pencil, he may copy the various figures in Plate IX. on a larger scale, endeavouring to produce similar representations of ground. When he can do this well, let him copy the same figures with a pen on the same scale as the plate; a little labour bestowed on this preliminary study will be more than repaid by the facility he will have acquired in representing the ordinary features of the earth's surface.

Fig. 1. Plate IX., shews the lines which should be first drawn, if the student were sketching a piece of ground similar to that represented in Fig. 3. The second figure shews the quantity of work which should be put on the field-sketch, to be afterwards finished in the manner shewn by the third figure, or with lines corresponding to the horizontal contour lines (and therefore not *crossed* as in the sketches in Plates X. and XI).

He should commence his field-work in a road

near the banks of the stream, the angle of a wood or any other remarkable feature. Taking a road for instance, he should start from a conspicuous point, and mark it on his paper. From this point he should trace faint lines in the direction of all objects of consequence which he can see, such as houses, remarkable trees, steeples, mills, &c., and on the lines so traced put the distance in paces that he conceives the near objects to be from him. Then looking along the line of road which he has to sketch, as far as his eye will reach with precision, and selecting a convenient object to be another point on the paper, he should estimate the distance it may be from him, and having put it down according to his scale, which scale may be notched on his pencil, he should pace the ground. Having ascertained the exact distance, and corrected any errors, the road should be permanently inserted on the sketch. From the second point a fresh start to a third should be taken, proceeding as before, and also again laying down the directions of the objects previously marked down, so as to find their positions by the intersection of the lines of direction, thus forming a net-work of triangles, and correcting the positions of the different objects selected as the prominent features in the sketch.

He should next proceed to sketch the slopes. For this purpose he must observe the positions of the top and bottom of each slope, and trace the crests of the hills as well as the bottom of the valleys and remarkable features. He should then estimate his distances by the eye to the extremities of the slopes, and sketch accordingly, correcting his judgment by measurement as often as he can. He should be very particular in noting whether each slope is practicable for the movements of infantry, of cavalry, or artillery, and at what pace cavalry may ascend without incapacitating the horses for further and immediate exertion.*

As soon as he can sketch accurately on foot, he should proceed to sketch on horseback, having previously ascertained the length of his horse's paces, both in walking and trotting.

Practice will give expedition, keeping in mind that errors can alone be corrected by measurement, and the observation of things in the same line, or nearly intersecting each other. For further details the article on "Field Sketching," in the "Aide Memoire to the Military Sciences," may be consulted.

The second species of sketching is partly based upon information collected from deserters, spies, people of the country, &c.; and to obtain greater

* The marks commonly used to denote whether or not the ground or road, &c., be practicable for artillery, cavalry, or infantry, are inserted in plate IX.

accuracy, and save time, there should be several officers to sketch the ground, while the troops accompanying them keep the enemy at bay. Whatever number are employed, the senior makes the arrangement, allotting to each his portion, while he collects and combines the whole of the results.

In these sketches the distances are to be marked on the roads, &c., calculated in paces of a man or horse ; and the time required for any specified troops—infantry or cavalry—to pass from one point to another in wet and dry weather should be noted.

It is obvious, in the third case, that the sketch will probably be made in a hasty manner, and that information must be added in writing to explain it ; the person making it should state in a conspicuous part what degree of dependence can be placed on its accuracy, how much he has himself seen, and what he has related on the information of others.*

* During the Peninsular war, an officer was ordered to sketch the left bank of the Douro, from Tordesillas downwards, when the British army retreated to Rueda, previous to the battle of Salamanca ; but as the enemy followed up the retreat very briskly, he could accomplish little else than what he saw as he galloped away from the advance of their cavalry. It was, however, necessary to present a sketch, and he wrote, in a large hand, across the face of it, " This sketch has no pretensions to accuracy, either as to bearings or distances." The superior officer to whom it was presented exclaimed. " Then of what use is it ?—you might as well

The last kind is a sketch of a province, department, &c. Of many countries maps exist that may be enlarged and completed to answer the purpose, taking care to correct all visible errors, and putting in as much detail as the scale will admit without causing confusion. If no such map can be had, or those possessed are two inaccurate, the resource is, either to make a rough series of triangles, observing the angles with a pocket sextant, having the exterior edge of its case divided like a protractor, with a small hole in the centre to place over the station, taking church-spires, windmills, obelisks, tops of hills, crags, single trees, &c., &c., as stations. Or, if the country be level and wooded, so that remarkable objects cannot be seen from each other, by taking the bearings along the roads, as far as can be seen, with the pocket compass, having its exterior limb divided as a protractor, and measuring the distances by pacing.

These instruments, with an ivory scale about 8 inches long, having scales of 4, 3, 2 and 1 inches on it, pen, ink, and pencil, are all that will be have been asleep!" The *culprit* could only state the fact that it was all he could do, and he was resolved to deceive no one. Even galloping sketches have their uses, for the one in question pointed out that there was a practicable road in that direction, showed the ravines and rivulets that crossed it, the nature of the ground over which it passed, and gave a rough idea of the distances.

necessary for laying down the skeleton map; but a good telescope is also very useful.

A field-sketch may be very accurately and expeditiously made with the aid of a Schmalcalder compass. Then it is only necessary to ascertain with care the length of any one line from the ends of which two or more remarkable objects may be discovered. The officer having laid down those points, determined by bearings taken with the compass at each end of that line, should proceed to any point where two of the objects so determined are to be seen; then taking their bearings, and protracting them on his paper, he will have determined his position, and can sketch the ground in his neighbourhood; he should then move to another spot, which he determines in like manner, by the intersection of bearings, and proceeds as before.

The angles taken should be noted down, but by having a scale and protractor always in the field, the operator is enabled to set off the angles or bearings, and lay down the distances at the moment he has ascertained them; and in addition to performing more by this method than any other, he will have the advantage of making the work complete as far as he has gone. In bad weather, when little can be done out of doors, the angles may be laid down more accurately, if necessary, on other paper, a supply of which, faintly ruled with parallel lines, should always be at hand. This skeleton map can be filled in at once, or this may be deferred to the last.

Plans of this nature have been occasionally executed without instruments; a few individuals, after a long life of practice, will effect this; but generally speaking, time is saved, and greater accuracy insured, by using instruments.

257. A reconnoissance is the process of examining a country, of which sketching is the delineation.

It is an operation which enables one to judge accurately of the advantages and disadvantages of ground with regard to military movements.

Military reconnoissances are made under circumstances similar to those already detailed in the first part of art. 246, as applicable to sketches and may be classed under the same heads.

258. The first class of reconnoissance consists in examining the nature of roads, to ascertain whether they are practicable for all, or only some species of troops, and their equipage; whether any and what repairs may be necessary; or whether it may not be more convenient to take other routes and avoid them entirely.

In ascertaining the size and position of the towns, villages, mills, chateaux, houses, &c., along the line of route, and what accommodation* they

* In cantoning troops permanently men should never be

afford for troops, either for a lengthened or a limited period; what fuel, water, provisions, forage, and means of transport of all kinds, can be procured in their neighbourhood; their salubrity or otherwise, and the principal occupations of the inhabitants; the lines of rivers and canals, and to what purposes they may be turned for the transport of troops, cannon, stores, or provisions; also the best ground for forming encampments; and, in addition to these, the reconnoitring officer should make such remarks as he thinks may in any way benefit the service to which he belongs.

The reconnoisance of the road from Truxillo to Merida (Plate X.), made on the 1st May, 1809, is a sufficient guide and form.

Much depends upon the knowledge previously obtained of the country which is to be the seat of

lodged singly: two at least must be together, and no house that cannot afford this can be made available. Families are not to be unnecessarily deprived of kitchen, bed-rooms in reason, and, if opulent, one retiring room.

Large farms may be rated for the keep of five horses—small ones two. In quartering troops for a night only, five men may be allowed per house in small towns and moderate sized villages; and in making the calculation for others, the numbers are to be increased or diminished according to circumstances. This arrangement includes officers and staff. Regiments and corps should be told off to adjacent streets, to keep the men in hand. For the same reason, it is preferable even to crowd the regiment, or brigade, into one village or town, rather than have them scattered through several, though the accommodation may be greater.

war. An obstacle overlooked may prove an impediment to the march of cavalry, or artillery, or even of large bodies of infantry; may derange a combined movement, nullify a projected simultaneous attack, and lead to the most disastrous results. Too much pains, therefore, cannot be taken in reconnoitring ground where the fate of nations is to be decided. To assist in these researches, it is prudent to take men belonging to the country, likely to possess, from their pursuits perfect knowledge of its localities. The best guides, are, therefore, gamekeepers, foresters, shepherds, poachers, smugglers, and wood-cutters. The greater number of these employed the better; they should be kept apart, and be examined separately; magistrates, too, must be examined, and made responsible for their answers.

But, as the information afforded by such persons is generally through compulsion, or for high rewards, it is not only to be regarded with the most jealous eye, but verified, when possible, by close inspection; or, at any rate, by minutely questioning the parties, to ascertain if any and what discrepancies may exist in their accounts.

Much useful knowledge may be derived as to the houses in towns and villages, and the disposition of the inhabitants, from clergymen, tax-gatherers, and inn-keepers. Let no officer despise information derived from any quarter; but at the same time be cautious how he receives it as true, or if true, whether he should not regard it as an exception to a general rule.*

259. In reconnoitring an enemy's position which forms the second object of our inquiry, it is necessary, 1st, to ascertain the extent of ground he occupies, and, if possible, the position of his reserves, in order to estimate the number of men he can bring into action.

2ndly. The situation of his batteries, whether in position or in field-works.

3rdly. If there be not in his line of defence towns, villages, country-houses, rivers, &c., that may augment his powers of resistance, or, on the contrary, facilitate an attack.

4thly. How his wings are covered or protected, and the time and route to be taken to turn them.

5thly. The roads, lanes, and even by-paths,

---

* The King of Prussia, in his "Instructions Secrètes," says, "There can be nothing more disgraceful to an officer than to make false reports, and, by way of exculpating himself, to say that he was deceived, or had not seen clearly. On these occasions, the officer must examine everything with the greatest care, have a clear conception and view of his subject, and be provided with a good telescope. Nothing should intimidate him; every difficulty should be surmounted. He will then be certain of what he has to report, and will not take a hundred horsemen for a regiment, or a flock of sheep for a corps of infantry, which often happens, however."

leading to his position, the bridges or fords to be passed, the works and time required to render them practicable; the boats, rafts, or other means to be employed to hasten or insure a passage, should rivers of consequence intervene.

6thly. Every height, ravine, hollow way, wood, copse, enclosure, wall, or hedge, that may cover the advance from his view and from the effect of his projectiles, or enable him to place an ambuscade.

7thly. The country in rear of his position,* if possible, so that, if dislodged, the end proposed in attacking him may be immediately attained, whether it be forcing him to manœuvre to disadvantage, cutting his line of operations, compelling him to retreat, or destroying his army entirely.

The officer to perform this service should be mounted on a strong serviceable horse, trained to leap, and steady under fire. Let him look well to his horse's shoes before he mounts, and not only carry a spare set with nails, &c, but learn how to put them on. It is easily done when the shoe fits the foot, by striking the nail straight and steadily, having given the point a slight bend

---

* During the night previous to the battle of Vimiera, the French patrolled between the British position and the seashore; their object probably was to make a reconnoissance.

outwards. The sabre-tache should be attached to the saddle by a couple of slings, *not* to the sword-belt, and should hold his sketch-book, the best map of the country he can obtain, prepared skin for drawing, pencils, ink-bottle, &c., counterbalancing a bag on the other side of the saddle containing his horse-shoes and as many feeds of corn as he can procure and carry without causing delay. A loaf cut in pieces, with a bottle of wine spilled upon it, is an excellent substitute for a feed of corn. A little starving will not hurt the officer, but his horse must not want. His instructions should be kept in a secret pocket in the waistband of his trousers.

An officer, while reconnoitring close to his position, or in an open unoccupied country, may sketch and make his remarks in safety; but it is very different when in the presence of an enemy, or on ground where woods, hills, ravines, &c., cover his advanced pickets and patrols. In the latter case, the reconnoisance must be protected by a force, large or small, according to the importance attached to its object, and the resistance expected to be met with. The officer should proceed then with the greatest precautions, and should be always accompanied by his scouts, to examine the villages, hollow ways, and woods. If he have both infantry and cavalry, he will dispose them according to the ground; in open country covering his infantry with cavalry, and in a close country the reverse. As much for their safety, as to preserve order in his force, he will at night place his cavalry between two detachments of infantry, of which the strongest will lead if he advance, and close his march when he retires, the whole force being preceded or followed by a few mounted men as scouts. The reconnoitring officer should, while advancing, remark what woods, marshes, bridges, ravines, villages, and gardens, &c., may be taken advantage of on his return, and pre-determine the disposal of his force, in the event of his retreat being impeded by the enemy. Independent of these important precautions, he will avoid dividing his force into smaller bodies, unless it may be at a moment when no inconvenience can result, and in the following cases— first, either to go himself, or send an officer, or trustworthy non-commissioned officer, into a village for information, where it may be unnecessary to take his whole force. Secondly, to make them "crown" heights, whence they may discover or verify what he is charged with reconnoitring. And, lastly, in the hope of acquiring further information by going beyond the exact point where his reconnoissance should cease but in this case he must take measures to support them until their object be obtained, when they will fall rapidly back on the main body.

He will not, however, pass any rising* ground within his reach without at least sending one man to its summit, or, if necessary, going himself; and he must not forget, that unless it be an extraordinary distance, no halt whatever can be permitted until the object of his mission be accomplished.

* Two dragoons will perform this service. They should separate when within a hundred yards of the summit, one pushing on to the top at a hand-gallop, the other following steadily after. When the leading dragoon, selected for his good sight, crowns the height, he should shade his eyes with his hand, and throw his glance rapidly, first round his immediate neighbourhood, then extend it to a distance. If all be right, let him inform his companion, or commanding officer, if within sight, by holding up his hand, or some other signal previously agreed upon. The other trooper then joins him, and after examining the ground together, they convey their information either by signal or returning to the party.

A soldier makes an excellent telegraph with his arms extended; thus—

 Enemy in force retiring.

 Enemy in force, advancing.

 Enemy on the right, advancing.

 Enemy on the left retiring.

and so on, varying the gestures according to the various circumstances.

In general he should avoid fighting. If, however, an enemy's detachment or post occupy a point which is necessary to be known, as much for itself as for what may be in its neighbourhood, and which may be rapidly forced without compromising his retreat, or leading prematurely to a general action, he will not hesitate to attack it, but with as much prudence and vigour as rapidity.*

If there should be an indispensable necessity for halting while within the enemy's reach, he will never make it at the extreme point to which he has gone, but after having returned at least a quarter of the way back to his own army; neither should he halt in a village, but choose high ground, whence he may discover anything that may be attempted against him, and where the approaches are difficult and the retreat easy. In all cases he will show a front of action towards the enemy, and though giving the required rest,

---

* "If it be desired to get possession of a height feebly occupied by the enemy, it must be approached secretly, and ascended with the greatest possible activity. The reconnoissance made, he should retire speedily, and by the most sheltered routes."—*Instructions Secretes, by Frederick the Great.*

The king then proceeds to show how the enemy may be deceived, and the best retreat made, which does not appertain to the subject now before us, but ought to be carefully studied by every officer, to whatever service he may belong, as a brief but excellent essay on outpost duties.

have half his men always ready to fight, establishing small advanced posts, and videttes, with strict injunctions to keep a sharp look out; and if required, he will have what provisions and forage may be necessary brought from the nearest village.

During the night he must be doubly viligant. As the chief part of the information to be collected must come from the inhabitants, a knowledge of the language is indispensable.

He should likewise know something of the country beforehand, from maps and books, that he may be able to judge of it at the first view, and to see at once, and clearly, everything that may turn to the advantage of the army with which be serves, or what, if not foreseen and prepared against, may obstruct its movements.

Roads.

260. In a reconnoissance the greatest attention must be paid to the roads. Notes should be made of their direction—width at different places, whether the same throughout or variable—their nature, whether paved, stony, through sand, clay, chalk, or over rock—even, or full of ruts, or liable to become soon damaged by the passage of troops, guns, or wagons; whether springs, streams, or other causes, may not render them partially or entirely impassable, and in what manner they may most readily be made available;

the material at hand, whether fascines,* hurdles, bundles of straw, or reeds, timber, or stone walls easily levelled, &c., the number of workmen and time required for this purpose. Whether the road may be used temporarily or permanently, or whether it may not be easier to form a new road near the old one, by levelling fences and filling up ditches; whether, if the road run across the breast of a hill, it be not exposed in certain seasons to slips of soil, which is frequently the case when there is a stratum of sand; whether bounded by hedges, trees, banks, or ditches. Its undulations, if liable to be enfiladed by the enemy's works, and what means may be taken to prevent it—if exposed, at certain turnings, to his view or fire—and how, and with what, a traverse or epaulment may be advantageously constructed—the time it will take to pass it—the

---

* As the principal difficulty in temporary roads consists in passing marshy or swampy ground, they may be made passable by laying down fascines, planks, or even round timbers. When fascines are used, if the road be covered with water, or is very soft, a row of fascines should be laid across the road, and on that a row lengthwise, and then again a third row above both, of smaller fascines, bound by twigs or withes, in the direction of the first row, the whole covered with earth or rubbish. Long grass, reeds, or rushes, may be used in the same way, tied in bundles. Bread-bags filled with grass, hay, chaff, straw, heath, furze, or any other such matter, will do; also, faggots of furze, covered with earth, gravel, or whatever is at hand.

small and high roads meeting it—whence they come, and whither they lead—and on what points troops may be judiciously placed in the neighbourhood to cover the force passing along it.

Military roads* should be 20 feet in breadth, and ought never to be less than 16 feet, unless in cases of emergency, when 8 may do.

Defiles.

261. Their dimensions, their direction, whether straight or curved, what forms the sides and bottom, whether rocky or sandy, lined with trees or brushwood, if easily blocked up, enfiladed, or defended by the enemy's light infantry. If it be absolutely necessary to pass through the defile, or whether other routes may not be chosen to avoid it. How cavalry are to pass, whether by squadrons, divisions, threes, twos, or single file—infantry, whether by companies, subdivisions, sections, or threes. If practicable for field-artillery, ammunition-wagons, and convoys. If the ground at its extremity be favourable for deploying. If

* During the late war, artillery and carriages of all kinds were, in many instances, brought over rugged and mountainous countries, were there was no trace of roads; in fact the operation of moving them in such situations must have been seen to be believed.

Most assuredly, the officers of the British artillery who served in the Peninsula were unrivalled in *zeal, abilities,* and *devotion to their duties*; and where such is the case, difficulties, obstructions, and even apparent impossibilities, vanish before them.

the defile, or part of it, can be used to screen reserves from the enemy's view or fire. The means to be employed, and the number of artificers requisite, to clear away natural obstacles or those which the enemy may have placed to obstruct a passage. The distance from, and names of, the nearest towns and military positions.

Bridges.

262. Their dimensions, materials, and constructions; the communications they establish; the readiest modes of destroying them if hurtful, or repairing them if the reverse, or to construct others; whether the latter operation may not be the most easy, from the facilities presented by the banks, &c., (which should also be critically examined, and accurately described.)

What means the enemy has of defending the bridges, and what points may be advantageously occupied by artillery, light infantry, &c., to cover the attacking party in their advance or retreat. If adapted to all, or only to certain descriptions of troops, and, as in defiles, with what extent of front these troops may cross; if they can deploy when arrived on the opposite side; and whether other passages may not be found shorter, or less exposed to observation or fire. The means at hand, or requiring to be transported, and the number of men and tools, &c., required to repair the work in case of accidents arising either from the superincumbent pressure, the effects of the enemy's shot, sudden floods, or floating ice or timber, or, as has in many instances happened, from large rafts, fire-boats, &c.*

* That part of the bridge at St. Jean de Luz which was constructed of timber was fired by the French in a very ingenious manner, to stay the British pursuit. When the British advance reached the bridge about seven o'clock A.M., the first bay, or interval between the bank and nearest upright frame-work supporting the superstructure, was so far consumed as to render new beams and planks necessary before any passage could be effected. The repair was commenced immediately, and completed in about an hour and a half, when the second bay was discovered to be on fire, and so far damaged as to require renewal. The officer employed, while his men were repairing this also, carefully examined the under side of the remaining bays; but as the beams supporting the road-way were planked underneath as well as above, nothing appeared that gave the least indication of these being injured. The repair of the second bay was completed about ten o'clock, and a considerable portion of infantry passed. In about an hour and a half afterwards, the third bay was discovered to be on fire, and so far damaged as to be considered unsafe. While the repair of the third bay was in progress, the remaining bay was partly unplanked, to see if the cause of this combustion, at periods varying from one and a half to three hours apart, could be discovered. Between the top and bottom planks, three boxes, about 2 feet long and 9 inches wide and deep, were found, containing a fuel, already so far decomposed by ignition that we could not ascertain its nature; and had we not discovered and removed them, this space would also have been consumed. The enemy's intention, in which they completely succeeded, was, it would appear, to destroy the different bays at inter-

Fords.

263. Their position—the marks which indicate them, the depth, length, and width—the volume and velocity of the water—and if it can by any means be suddenly augmented, to render the passage impracticable. If exposed to the enemy's fire, and how that fire may be silenced or rendered useless—the roads leading to and from the ford—what chance there might be of the enemy's attacking while passing it, and from what quarter—if passable for infantry, cavalry, guns, or convoys, or for all—the nature of the soil forming the bed—whether likely to be rendered impracticable by heavy rains or melting snow, or, if near the mouth of a river, what effect the rise and fall of the tide produce upon it.

A ford should not be deeper than 3 feet for infantry, 4 feet for cavalry, and $2\frac{1}{2}$ feet for artillery and ammunition-waggons.

If a ford be situated where the current is rapid, its depth should be diminished in proportion, from $\frac{1}{2}$ foot to 1 foot for cavalry, and from 9 inches to $1\frac{1}{2}$ feet for infantry.

Having reconnoitred a ford, it will be prudent

vals, that we might not discover the extent of the injury all at once, and prepare the necessary means of repair for the whole; and doubtless they gained, by so doing, several hours more time to get out of the way.

This account is supplied by the officers of the Staff Corps charged with repairing the bridge.

to plant upright pickets in the stream, notched to show the variations of the depths at different times. In mountainous countries these variations will be considerable in winter. The line marked should be such as to avoid the large stones frequently found in fords among hills, rendering the passage difficult for cavalry and impossible for carriages.

In sandy countries, and where alluvial deposits are frequent, fords may be found which are fit for infantry in small numbers, but impracticable for cavalry and for carriages—sometimes appearing to have a firm and solid bed, but proving, on critical examination, soft or shifting.* The best

---

* The passage of the Bidassoa, in 1813, effected by part of the left column of the British army, is an example, in this branch of reconnoitring, which will teach more than any detailed rules. The officer employed to examine the fords thus writes to the author:—

"I found a great deal of difficulty in ascertaining the existence of any fords at all below the Irun bridge; and all the information I got, proved, in the sequel, incorrect. The river is made up of a number of mountain torrents, and, when in flood, is charged with such a quantity of sand that if it chances to be repelled by a gale of wind at the same time, a bar, or sand-bank, is thereby formed, which serves the purposes of a ford until the next flood and storm remove it to some other place. The lower one of these, opposite the town of Fontarabia, where General Hay's brigade passed, I discovered accidentally. I was watching the enemy constructing a battery below this place on their own side, and hearing shots, turned my glass to the quarter whence the sound came, and saw two men running as fast as they could towards the river—the French

have a gravelly bottom. Great care must be taken in the examination of fords across streams or rivers threading a morass or boggy district. A brown rushy bottom may generally be trusted, but bright green spots are delusive.

For these reasons no points under military reconnoissance, particularly when an attack is contemplated, require more accurate knowledge than

picket firing at them. The men reached the water apparently unhurt; and, to my surprise, walked across, not more than waist-deep, at least I thought so, although they kept ducking to avoid the shot from the French. I galloped to meet them; but they escaped me, as I was delayed by the intersection of great drains and embankments in the water meadows. Probably they were Spanish peasants who had been detained by the French, and were regaining their liberty. Having thus ascertained the existence of one ford, I set myself to work to verify what I had seen, and try and find another, in which I also succeeded, higher up than Fontarabia.

"As to the troops having time to do anything *after* they crossed, and *before* the return of the tide, *they had none.* We crossed at low water, and in *twenty minutes* there was such an influx as would have prevented a re-passage. In fact, I myself (who was obliged to gallop two miles off, to start the brigade that passed higher up, and who had not seen our signal) found the water so deep on my return as to float myself and my horse. The bottom was very bad, being a moveable sand. Our object was to get across and join the troops that passed above us. The attack was simultaneous along the whole position. The enemy was greatly surprised, and rapidly retired to *concentrate* on the heights in the rear, leaving the communication along the river clear to us."

fords; and no excuse whatever should exonerate a reconnoitring officer from not having *personally* examined and sounded them.

A row of pickets planted on either side of the ford, and retained by cordage will be found useful, as well in the crossing as for the indication of its direction. When a ford is of sufficient width, and the stream is rapid, it is sometimes expedient for the cavalry to cross so as to cut the current of water obliquely, and to make the infantry cross lower down.

When columns of attack composed of different arms are pushed across a ford of sufficient width, and the ground on the enemy's side admits of their deploying immediately for a charge, the infantry should pass in the centre, and the cavalry on either side covered by the fire of artillery. The infantry will, when arrived at the opposite bank, throw out skirmishers, and forming as they come up, push on to support them. The cavalry will move steadily through the water, deploy without confusion on the flanks, and endeavour by a vigorous charge, to drive the enemy as far back as possible, to allow the remainder of the troops to pass the river without molestation.

Woods and Forests.

264. These may have great effect on the successes or reverses of a campaign. They should

be examined accurately as to their position and dimensions; the sort of trees of which they are composed, whether of forest trees, copse, or underwood—if of large timber, furnished with branches to the ground, which, blending with underwood, form a good cover for light infantry, or standing far apart, the ground being only covered with grass, and permitting cavalry to penetrate—if occupied by the enemy, and by what description of troops—if in front of his position, what advantage he may derive from being enabled thereby to conceal his advanced posts, and if this appears to have been done, whether it is easiest to drive them out by turning their flanks, or cut them off by at once pushing between them and his main body—if in the line of his position, how they may cover his reserves, and if, instead of protecting, they hinder the communication, and prevent his different corps affording mutual assistance and co-operation—and if in rear of his position, whether the woods or forest may not prove points to retire upon, from which it will take time and trouble to expel him.

As this species of reconnoissance is attended with great personal risk, some use must necessarily be made of the information of people belonging to the neighbourhood. They should be examined particularly (paying liberally for true reports, and vigorously punishing those who have supplied false information) about the roads and paths leading through them, and if ravines, rivulets, or marshes are to be met with either in, or bordering on, them. It will be also necessary to know to what account the timber may be turned, whether it will furnish the materials for making fascines, hurdles, palisades, abatis, &c., for repairing carriages, laying bridges, &c. Single trees, and remarkable edifices, gable ends of houses, spires, high chimneys, and other isolated objects that fix the attention, and serve to indicate certain points either for the alignment, or direction, of a column of troops, or advantageous as positions for advanced posts or artillery, should be carefully noted.

Hedges and Ditches.

265. Hedges are generally thin and poor in sandy soils, but are often impenetrable in stiff soil. They should be examined with attention, lest they prove serious checks in an attack, hide an enemy's sharpshooters, mask his batteries, or, if substantial and protected by a tolerable ditch in front, and a low wall or bank, form an entrenchment. A reconnoitring officer will, therefore, report upon their general height (supposing their position is of consequence), of what composed, and if simply rising out of the ground, or combined with ditches, &c., which render them

obstacles of importance. The depth and nature of the latter must also be noted.

Rivers, Streams, and Canals.

266. These are to be carefully examined. If navigable, by what description of vessels, and what those vessels will hold—the velocity per hour of the current—what rapids, eddies, rocks, &c., present themselves—the banks, nature, and configuration of the soil—if protecting an enemy's front or wings—the best means of crossing, whether with boats, pontoons, rafts, &c.,—whether the points of passage are much exposed, and how they may be covered and defended—if near the sea, what influence the tide may have—the depth and breadth at various times of tides and floods.*

---

* When the allied army occupied the country south of Bayonne, in the spring of 1814, the head quarters being at St. Jean de Luz, it was proposed to construct a bridge across the Adour, below Bayonne, for the left of the army to cross in the first instance, and afterwards to keep up the communication with the rear, leaving a force to invest the town, which is situated at the confluence of the Adour and Nive, three miles from the sea, it being judged inexpedient to delay advancing the main body of the army after the reduction of the fortified camp, town and citadel.

Two officers of the Royal Staff corps, one of whom has supplied this account and sketch, were directed to proceed from St. Jean de Luz to make their way between the front of the French camp and the sea, to observe if there existed any natural obstruction to the construction of the bridge, in the first instance; to fix the most eligible situation for it; to ascertain the

FIELD FORTIFICATION.   293

With reference to the latter, it should be specified how and when they come down; as snow breadth of the river at the spot determined on; and to suggest what precautions might be necessary to counteract any attempts of the enemy from the town, by floating heavy vessels, fire-rafts, or anything else, down by the ebb-tide to destroy it.

They started from the English outposts with an escort of a sergeant and four dragoons, the object being concealment; and proceeding by the dotted line, reached the mouth of the river at A without being observed; but there being a guard at B on the opposite bank, it became necessary to retire a little to avoid being seen. They then proceeded through straggling pine-trees, which, however, afforded a good cover, towards D, leaving a dragoon to watch the house C, where there was a small picket, and sending the sergeant, with the two other dragoons, towards the position E, retaining only

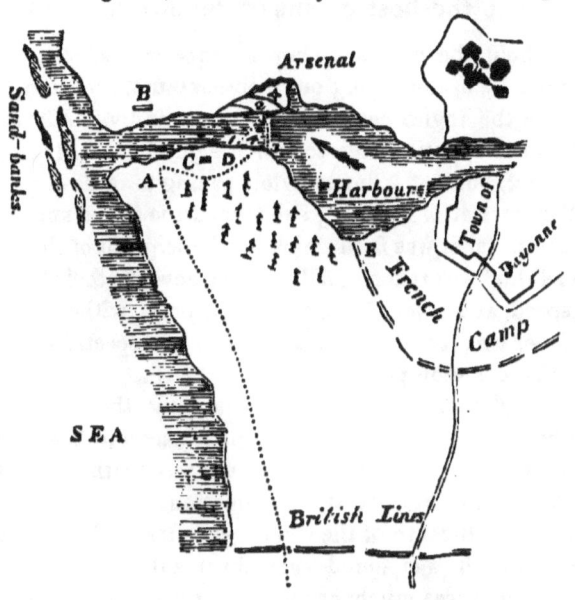

melting many miles off, periodical rains, letting off waters used for irrigation, &c., may materially increase the volume and force of the water just at the very moment when columns of attack may be formed for crossing, or during their passage, or, worse still, when a part only of the force has crossed over.

Canals and water-courses should be examined as to the best means of drawing off the water in other directions, using or destroying them for navigable purposes, deepening their beds, or repairing their banks, so as to carry off artificial inundations made by the enemy. The positions of lock and sluice-gates should be accurately laid down, also the best means of destroying them, and

one to hold the horses. They at once walked out on the wharf wall 1 3, and taking out their sextants, simultaneously observed the angles between each other individually and a post on the opposite bank to which a gun boat was fastened, viz., 1 3 2, and 3 1 2, immediately pacing towards each other till they met at 4. Having exchanged the above angles and distances, a shot was fired which hit the sergeant of the escort, who fell and was taken. All the rest now put their horses to full speed, and reached their own outposts without further loss; nor was it ever said that the enemy suspected anything beyond a common patrol.

The object of the officers exchanging the angles and lengths of lines forming the triangle to ascertain the breadth of the river was that, in case one should meet with an accident, the other might have all the information.

When the breadth of the river was afterwards accurately ascertained, it was found that the result of this hurried measurement was much nearer the truth than could have been expected.

FIELD FORTIFICATION. 295

the effect their destruction might produce. In countries where rivers feed canals, and are used for irrigation, the means of rendering them available, either by artificial inundation or damming up streams so as to create a flood at any particular moment, &c., should be noted and reported on, as conducive to the strength of a position.

Swampy Meadows, Marshes, Bogs.

267. Their position, dimensions, and origin, whether arising from land-springs, inundations of the sea, overflowing of a neighbouring river, or otherwise. How to be traversed, either by permanent or temporary roads. If there may not exist paths or roads little known, at the time disused, but capable of being put in a state of repair —if impassable, the best routes for avoiding them —also the nature of the surrounding country.

In sandy and heathery ground marshes exist in winter which are entirely dried up in summer. If old traces of wheels are here perceptible, they should be followed and the ground sounded, as the routes thus indicated may become essentially useful for the passage of troops.

Swampy meadows are generally impracticable for cavalry, and sometimes even for infantry. They are easily discovered by the aspect of their plants, usually rank grass among which is often seen a green and yellow moss. It may be remarked that certain plants indicate the nature of the soil, as well as the depth of water, and its constant presence.

Mountains, and Mountainous Districts.

268. Their position, if connected in a chain or isolated—their slopes, crests, the important points occupied by the enemy, and the best routes to be taken, either to turn or attack them (see *Roads*)— the nature of the soil—whether bare, in pasture, arable, or covered with wood. If it be possible, and how, an enemy pent up in a mountainous, and perhaps poor country may be cut off from his supplies, or the general line of his operations.

Whether precipices, ravines, torrents, or other obstacles, intervene to prevent his wings co-operating, or acting simultaneously, and what advantage may be taken of them. The relative commands* are to be judged of as accurately as the reconnoitring officer can, supposing he has not means of ascertaining them by measurement, and he will be careful in specifying what points may be advantageously occupied by artillery, light infantry, &c., while covering an attack, and where to place videttes, look-out posts, or telegraphs Should the enemy hold the crest of a range of

* These are generally marked on the sketch by figures, beginning at the lowest and proceeding upwards.

hills in force, with his wings so protected that it is absolutely necessary to dislodge him from his position nice discrimination is required to point out the line of the premeditated attack, particularly if the attacking force has first to descend a slope, cross a valley, and then mount the high ground he rests on; for during the descent, and whilst crossing the intervening hollow, there will be a complete exposure to his fire (if within his range), as well as a manifest exposition of the exact points intended to be assailed, and the force brought against them. Let the reconnoissance, therefore, be most carefully made from different points of view; that no inequality of the ground, whether advantageous to the enemy, or likely to impede his fire or line of sight, should be omitted in the sketch or remarks accompanying it.

Open Towns, Villages, Hamlets, Farm-Houses, and their Dependencies—Isolated Houses.

269. Their situation, and if of sufficient importance to occupy a prominent place in a line of operations—if calculated for holding a large force during a short period, or a small force permanently—if likely to be the quarters of outposts, pickets, &c., how they may be defended—the best means of attacking them—and, if carried, what benefit will result—the construction of the houses, the gardens, plantations, &c., that are in their vicinity

—the communication through, and the roads leading to and from the neighbouring country. Should the enemy be driven out, and endeavour to regain the position, the best means of repulsing him—of intrenching it—placing convoys there in safety, or forming a base for further operations.

For this last purpose, the number of inhabitants and houses* should be ascertained, the resources† in cattle, carriages, horses, corn, and forage; the workmen and workshops of all descriptions, bake-houses and mills, whether turned by wind or water, principal churches, or other buildings that may serve as magazines or hospitals, the quantity and quality of the supplies of water, and what materials may be found for the repair or construction of carriages, pontoons, harness, intrenching tools, arms, &c. Should a small town, hamlet, or village, be occupied by an enemy in front of his line, in all probability he has rendered it as strong as he can, by palisades, barricades, overturned wagons, ditches, loop-holed houses and garden-walls, abatis, &c.; he will also have a good look-out from the church steeple, or tops of the highest houses to prevent surprise. It will, therefore, require some sagacity, and a good deal of boldness, to reconnoitre his position accurately. It may

* In Roman Catholic countries these are readily obtained from the priest.
† These from the magistrates.

be possible to approach under cover of hedges, copses, garden-walls, &c., close enough to see what he is about without being discovered by his videttes or patrols; at the dawn of day a rapid view may be had from the top of a neighbouring tree, or after dusk an individual possessed of coolness and presence of mind may crawl unperceived close up to his defences, remark their nature, and even overhear the conversation going on within; but it is sometimes necessary to make a false attack on one point to draw attention from an opposite point where the reconnoissance may be proceeding. This attack should be made with the utmost vivacity and uproar; and the moment the object in view is attained, a retreat should be executed with equal celerity.

Sea Coasts.

270. In addition to the various details of which we have treated, and which must be accurately examined along the sea-coast as elsewhere, we are to consider the sea as also susceptible of becoming the theatre of war. A reconnoitring officer will therefore, sketch and report upon the nature and configuration of the coast—the bays, harbours, creeks, roadsteads, and anchorages—whether accessible at certain, or at all times of tide, with only some or all winds—what batteries, redoubts, fortified buildings, may command land-

ing places—what woods or inequalities of ground are likely to hold an enemy concealed until the moment of disembarkation, when a certain degree of confusion always exists—if bordered by cliffs their height and shape—if by sandy beach or mud, the extent thereof at low water, how near vessels may lie with safety*—what sort of boats are chiefly used by the coasters, pilots, fishermen, &c.—and what times of tide are most favourable for the debarkation of troops, &c.

A reconnoitring officer should distinguish those parts of his report drawn from personal examination from those collected from other sources, which he may not have an opportunity of verifying.

Great lakes are often important military features. Provisions, reinforcements, &c. &c., may be forwarded by them. It is therefore very necessary to ascertain what creeks, harbours, &c. &c., exist where shipments of men or stores may be made—the depth of water, &c. &c.—whether the points of embarkation and debarkation be susceptible of defence, and present ground on which troops can easily deploy.

In the third species of reconnoissance, an officer charged with finding a position most capable of checking the advance of an enemy, or

* This comes more properly under the head of maritime surveying, but nothing should be omitted in a reconnoissance.

offering him battle, has, first, to consider the face of the country with a view of placing troops under cover by natural or artificial means, by taking advantage of defences already existing, or constructing forts, redoubts, lines, &c., where they may be required; secondly, to avoid ground where the enemy may approach with an extended front; and thirdly, to make sure that there are convenient communications in rear of the position, to preserve the line of operations, and enable the component parts of the army to afford mutual and effectual co-operation and support.

It does not always happen that ground exactly suitable can be found if a retreat, instead of an advance, becomes unavoidable, but advantage must be taken of the best that presents itself, recollecting that everything which before seemed favourable to an enemy, and in the way of an attacking army, will then be, in general, disadvantageous, must be examined carefully, and be turned to the best account, or destroyed, if possible.

According to these principles, a position should be selected calculated for the number of troops who are to occupy it, neither tending to cramp their exertions by diminishing their field of action, nor, by extending them too much, weaken their effect.

There is little safety in a chain of small detached posts.* By their occupation an army is broken into advanced guards and pickets—weak in many places, strong in none—easily broken through, beaten in detail, or perhaps avoided altogether. A strong rallying point is required, from which outposts, when attacked, may be reinforced, or where, if driven in they may find protection; where troops may feel themselves, by their position, more than on a par with superior numbers should they be attacked; where the component parts of the army are held well together, to act with effect when directed with a particular object by the individual who commands them. There should always be this strong point—this *key* of a position.

If the troops are to halt for any time on the ground to be defended, it will be necessary to take into consideration how they are to be supplied with water, fuel, and provisions, during their halt.

If the country be mountainous, or woody, and the front and flanks difficult of access, there should be an uninterrupted command of view and fire over the surrounding ground for at least 1200 yards, at which distance field-artillery will do good service, particularly if enfilading a column, or when the enemy cannot form his order of battle without being exposed to their effect.

* This was our misfortune at Albuera.

The flanks should rest on points, such as rivers, artificial inundations, fortified towns or villages, swamps, mountains, ravines, the sea-coasts, or impracticable forests, which cannot be turned by the enemy without making a considerable circuit, or a flank movement, which may expose him to an attack, or by abandoning his line of operations. Thereserves, and second line of battle, ought to be at least 600 yards in the rear of the first, that the regiments in their front may find no obstacle if required to move by the rear to any point in the line where their presence may be wanted.

Supposing the position taken up to be eventually carried by the enemy,* their success should not cause the destruction of the army. A position for defence may be good, but its rear may not present a single object to cover a retreat. A commanding officer must be hard pushed indeed when he determines to make a final stand. An action fought is seldom an end gained; it is only the means whereby ulterior views are attained; and it has not unfrequently happened, that the party worsted in fight has eventually been the gainer, while the actual conqueror in the field has, by his

---

* Our position at Waterloo had the forest of Soignies in the rear; and if the greater force of the Emperor had compelled us to retire on the 18th, before the appearance of the Prussians, the Duke would have maintained himself with his infantry, still covering Brussels, until they came up.

own inactivity immediately afterwards, his ignorance of the beaten army's further resources, of their subsequent movements, or perhaps by a rash and uncalculating pursuit, thrown away the advantages his victory should have ensured to him.

Therefore, in reconnoitring for a retreating army, not only one position should be accurately examined, but the next in the rear of it, where the army may concentrate again and defend itself, or where a part of it may retire, and maintain the ground until succour arrive, or, at least, till honourable terms can be procured.

The form of a report for an advancing or retreating reconnaissance may be the same as that already given on the road from Truxillo to Merida. An additional column, however, may in some cases be advantageously introduced between the "sketch of the road," and "places on the road and near it," with elevations of remarkable objects, rendering the report more graphic; and the "observations" may extend to these extra illustrations, or a particular column of remarks applicable to them be inserted, as circumstances require.

Particular positions on either side of the route are to be sketched and reported on separately, if of importance.

A plan of the country made from these sketches having the line of march of both armies laid down on it in different colours, with particular marks for the best positions, should accompany the reports of the reconnoissance made to the quarter-master-general of the army, who will probably direct the reconnoitering officer to sketch the routes for the different columns, whether advancing or retreating, to enable them to arrive together on a particular spot, either for encamping, for attack, or for defence. A form for the march of four columns is given in Plate XII., which will be a sufficient guide.

271. In making a general reconnoissance, the last division of our subject, the combined knowledge of the soldier, the naturalist, and the political economist, is required, to give a comprehensive description of its military position and communications, its resources, and the general pursuits, feelings, and interests of its inhabitants. But in days of general peace, when actual service occupies only a short part of our time and profession, we have more leisure for study, more incentives to acquire general knowledge than any other body of professional men. The pen and pencil have, during a long peace, superseded the sword, in making a way for him who wields them to honour and distinction.

We should then enter freely, fully, and heartily on our profession, first learning implicit obedience, that at a future period we may know how to command; and making ourselves masters, as opportunities are afforded, of chemistry, natural history, mechanics, and, above all, languages. A diplomatist is not more necessarily a linguist than a soldier is.

In a work of this description no particular instructions can be given for making a general reconnoissance, beyond what has been said under this head on sketching, and filling up the annexed form for methodising the operation; but an officer can only qualify himself for undertaking such a task by reading and making notes of what he reads; by observing the country through which he passes with a military eye, and by making the daily practice with his pen as much a point of duty as his attendance at parade.

APPENDIX.

NOTE I.

PROBLEMS, &c., RELATING TO THE SCIENTIFIC METHOD OF DEFILADING WORKS.

1. Having explained the practical methods of defilading field works, we shall now proceed to show in what manner they may be defiladed in the closet, with the aid of a plan only; a knowledge of which mode of defilading works is essential to the thorough understanding of the subject.

2. In the graphic operations relating to defilade, the outline of the proposed fortress or work is laid down on a plan, which should also contain all the ground within 2000 yards of the most advanced works, The vertical dimensions are indicated by numbers, or by scales, showing the distance of the several parts of the fortress, or of the ground, above or below a horizontal plane, called the *plane of comparison.*

In the following brief exposition of the problems relating to defilade, and their application, the plane of comparison has been assumed as passing *above* all the ground.

The ground is represented by horizontal contour lines, or sections, Fig. 64, made at equal vertical distances (generally one yard), and at the side of each contour a number is written, showing its distance below the plane of comparison.

If an inclined plane were represented in the manner above described, the horizontal sections would be parallel equidistant right lines $a\,a$, $b\,b$, &c., Fig. 62, the distance between these lines decreasing in proportion to the steepness of the plane; so that if the plane were vertical, all the horizontal sections would be projected under one line: the horizontal trace or projection of a vertical plane is therefore a right line.

3. Any line C D perpendicular to the horizontal sections of an inclined plane is evidently drawn in the direction of the greatest slope of that plane, and is divided into equal parts by the sections $a\,a$, $b\,b$, &c.: this line, so divided, is called the *scale of the plane*, and is used to represent the inclination of the plane to which it belongs.

The scale of a plane C D Fig. 66, being given, to find the height of any point O on the plane; let fall from the given point a perpendicular on the scale, and the intersection will show the height of the point required. A line A B is usually drawn perpendicular to the scale, and parallels to this line may afterwards be drawn from any points of which the heights are required. Previous to entering further on this subject, it is necessary to understand perfectly the following Problems.

4. PROBLEM I.—Three points in an inclined plane being given, to find the scale of inclination. Let A B and C; Fig. 67, be the given points, their distances below the plane of comparison being 16, 13, and 17 yards: join the three points by right lines A B, B C, and divide each line into as many equal parts as there are units of difference between the points

which terminate it, viz., A B into three, and B C into four equal parts; join any two similarly numbered parts, as H R: this line being equidistant from the plane of comparison at the two points H and R, must be horizontal, and being drawn on the plan, is, therefore, one of the horizontal sections of the given plane.

The scale of the plane is perpendicular to the horizontal sections (art. 3); draw then D E perpendicular to H R; and, to graduate it, draw parallels to H R through the divisions marked on either of the lines A B, B C. The line D E thus graduated is the scale sought.

5. PROBLEM II.—Given the scales of inclination of two planes, to find their intersection.

Case 1.—When the scales of inclination are not parallel.

Let A B, C D, Fig. 68, be the given scales. Draw horizontal lines through any two points, on one of the scales A B, similarly numbered, to two points on the other plane, and also through the corresponding points on the scale C D. The points of intersection of these lines being common to both the planes, if a line E F be drawn through them it will show the intersection required. If the opening of the angle formed by the horizontal sections be turned towards the ascending points of the scales, the line E F will form a ridge; if turned in the contrary direction, it will form a gutter or furrow. If it were required to find the intersection of a line with a plane, consider the line as the scale of a plane, and finding the intersection of the two planes, as already described, produce the given line to that intersection, which will evidently be the point where it will intersect the plane.

Case 2.—When the scales of inclination are parallel.

In this case, the horizontal lines drawn on the surfaces of the two planes being parallel, cannot intersect each other; but as the intersection of the planes must, therefore, be perpendicular to both scales, it will only be necessary to find one point of that intersection, which may be readily done by constructing vertical sections of both planes, in the following manner:—

Let CD, BA, Fig. 69, be the given scales; it may be at once seen that their intersection lies between the 15th and 19th divisions. Take any point on one side of the intersection (19), and draw horizontal lines through that point of division of both scales, making cd equal to 19 a; from a, draw a line to any point B 14, on the other side of the intersection; through the corresponding point of the other scale draw a horizontal line, intersecting the first scale in e; join de, the intersection of the lines a B, de will be the point sought; through which draw PL perpendicular to the given scales; the line PL is common to both the planes, and is the intersection required. The distance 19 a, may be taken of any convenient length.

6. PROBLEM III.—To find the intersection of an inclined plane with a given surface, represented by horizontal contours.

Let AB, Fig. 70, be the scale of the plane, and CDE the given surface; produce the horizontal sections of the plane until they cut the similarly numbered contours of the given surface; join the points of intersection $abcd$, &c., for the intersection required

The vertical distance between any point X, of the surface, and the section made by the plane is thus found:—From a given point let fall a perpendicular on the scale AB; now, the number corresponding to X on the surface is 14, and on the plane 14½; consequently the point X is half a yard above the section made by the plane. The difference of level between any number of points may be found in a similar manner, and data be obtained for calculating the volume of the mass cut off by the given plane.

7. PROBLEM IV.—To construct the section of a surface cut by a vertical plane.

Let AB, Fig. 71, be the horizontal trace of a vertical plane: then imagine it also to represent the plane of comparison in a vertical section; from the points of intersection of the line AB with the contours of the given surface, let fall perpendiculars a, b, c, d, &c., equal to the distances of those contours below the plane of comparison; a line drawn through the ends of the perpendiculars will shew the section required.* If the trace of the vertical plane were a right line, drawn in the direction A B, then it would be necessary to determine other intermediate points, in addition to the intersections of the vertical plane with the horizontal contours, to get a true representation of the section.

8. PROBLEM V.—To construct the intersection of a vertical plane with an inclined plane.

Let AB, Fig. 72, be the horizontal trace of the ver-

* In constructing sections formed by vertical planes, if the scale of the plan be so small as to render the differences of level not sufficiently apparent, any larger scale may be made use of to measure the vertical distances of the section.

tical plane; then suppose it to represent the plane of comparison in a vertical section; produce any two horizontal sections of a given plane till they intersect AB; from the points of intersection a and b, let fall perpendiculars ac, bd, equal to the distances of the sections used, below the plane of comparison; a line drawn through dc will show the required intersection.

9. PROBLEM VI.—To find a horizontal line in a plane, containing on its surface a given inclined line and forming with the horizon a given slope or angle.

Let AB, Fig. 73, be the given line, and suppose the perpendicular and base of the right-angled triangle which measures the slope to be 3 and 2.

At any point M, on the line A B, of a given height with a radius taken from the scale of the plan, equal to the base of the given triangle, describe a circle.

If we imagine the point M to be the summit of a cone three yards high, and the described circle to be its base, then the plane sought must evidently be a tangent to that cone. The base being three yards below the point M, find a point L on the given line, also three yards lower than M; from L draw a tangent to the base of the cone, and it will be a horizontal section of the plane sought.

Oblique scales are sometimes made use of, the divisions of which are required to be of a given length. To construct a scale of this description, draw a parallel to L T through any other division of the line A B; from any point P on this line, with a radius equal to the difference of level between the sections P and LT multiplied by the given length of each division of the oblique scale, describe an arc cutting the line L T; draw a line through P and the point so found, for the direction of the oblique scale required, which may then be graduated as in the figure. A horizontal line should always be drawn at one end of an oblique scale. This description of scale is made use of to represent the superior and exterior slopes of parapets.

10 PROBLEM VII.—To find the scale of a plane that shall contain on its surface a given right line, and be a tangent to a given surface.

Case 1.—When the given scale is inclined.

Let A B, Fig. 74, be the given line, and aaa, bbb, the given surface; draw tangents C E, D S, from the several points on the line A B, to the similarly numbered contours of the given surface. That tangent which forms with the given line the smallest angle on its descending side, will be a horizontal section of the plane required; draw D H parallel to C E, and a division of the scale of inclination is obtained. The smaller the angle is, which any one of the horizontal tangents forms with the given line, the steeper must be the plane which contains on its surface that tangent and that given line; and as the steepest plane must be taken in this case, it follows that the tangent which forms the smallest angle with the given line is the one by which the scale is determined.

If, instead of the tangent C E, the tangent D S were used to construct the scale, the plane thus found would cut off a portion of the given surface $a\ a\ a$, contained within the angle E C U, and would therefore not be a tangent to the given surface. This plane is called the *plane of site* or *regulating plane;* and the line A B *is the line of site*. It would often happen that, from the slight inclination of the given line, no numbers could be found on it corresponding to those on the contours to which tangents ought to be drawn ; in this case assume a point of contact, as *a* Fig. 75, and draw a line from that point to any division of the given line; graduate this line, and join a corresponding number on it and on the given line, for a horizontal section of the plane sought; construct the scale as in the figure; then, if one of the horizontal sections of the plane be not a tangent to a similarly numbered contour, while all the other sections leave the corresponding contours in front of them, assume a fresh point of contact, and proceed as before.

Case 2.—When the given line is horizontal.

11. Let A B, Fig. 76, be the given line, and suppose its distance below the plane of comparison to be 16 ; parallel to A B draw *a b*, *c d*, and *e f*, tangents to the contours of the given surface. If the line A B were moved forward, preserving its horizontal position, it would evidently touch the ground in the direction of the curve *v t s*, and coincide with each of the tangents *a b*, *c d*, *e f*, in succession; generating a cylindrical surface*, which we may suppose to be represented by the line A B and those several tangents. At any point C, in the line A B, draw C E

---

* If we imagined a line perfectly horizontal of indefinite length. not partaking of the curvature of the earth, and lying due north and south, to be moved round the earth on the equator, we should have a cylindrical surface generated of the same diameter as the earth, and if a similar line be anywhere on the surface of the earth, supposed to move in like manner on a great circle, it will necessarily form a portion of a nearly similar cylinder.

perpendicular to A B, and also from the same point any line C D. If we assume the line C E to be the trace of a vertical plane, construct a section of the cylindrical surface made by that vertical plane, and having projected the point C in the same section, draw thence a tangent to the section, and transfer the point of contact of the tangent and section to the line C E, we shall have a point in the plane tangent to the surface required.

Again, if we imagine C E and C D to be the two sides of a triangle, and that C E is a tangent to the cylindrical surface before described, it will evidently touch that surface in the same point or points, whatever the inclination of C D may be.

From C set off on C D as many equal divisions as may be necessary to shew its assumed inclination; join the points on the line C D with the similarly numbered points of contact of CE, and the tangents, $a\,b,\,c\,d$, and $e\,f$. The line which forms the smallest angle with C D, on the descending side of that line, will indicate the point of contact of C E with the cylindrical surface, and consequently one of the points of division of the scale sought.

12. PROBLEM VIII.—To find the scale of a plane which shall contain a given point, and be a tangent in two points to a given surface.

Let P, Fig. 77, be the given point, its distance from the plane of comparison being 8; from P draw lines P A, P A', &c.; then through P draw any other line P B, and mark divisions on it, to shew its assumed inclination. By proceeding in the manner described in Art. 11, we may find the points where the several lines P A, P A', &c., touch the given surface. Graduate all those lines, viz., divide each into as many parts as there are units of difference between its respective point of contact with the ground, and the given point P. The point P may then be conceived to be the apex of a solid angle, of which the lines P A, P A', are the ridges and furrows; make a horizontal section of this solid angle, *i.e.*, join a set of similarly numbered points on the ridges and furrows before mentioned, and draw tangents to the horizontal section so made: in the example there are three tangents C D, E F, and I R, any one of which may be taken as a horizontal section of the plane sought. That tangent which is most distant from the given point will give the plane of least inclination. If the horizontal section had presented only one salient angle towards the given point, a vast number of planes might have been found; in this case the one which most nearly coincides with the ground to be occupied by the works should be selected.

APPLICATION OF THE PRECEDING PROBLEMS, &c.,

13. In art 62 it is stated that the maximum of relief for the parapets of field fortifications is twelve feet. Let us suppose then, the base, or line of site of a work, to be horizontal, and let A B, Fig. 78, represent the plan of a vertical plane perpendicular to the line of site, meeting the surface of the ground in P, and forming the section P *m n*; let *c* be the point of contact of the same plane with the line of site, D E the vertical line corresponding to the salient angle of the proposed work, and *c g* the section of

the plane of site; the plane of defilade, being parallel to *c g*, would thus pass eight feet above the point of command.*

If *m f* exceed twelve feet, the relief of the salient will be greater than the maximum allowed. Another line of site must then be tried, which we shall still suppose horizontal, and meeting the vertical line in a point *h*, below the level of the ground; the section of the corresponding plane of site will be the line *h t*, and that of the plane of defilade the line *r s*. If *m v* be less than twelve feet, the new plane of sight will be within the required limits. This plane must necessarily cut the ground in a part of the exterior space near the gorge; there will, therefore, be a portion of that space from which the interior of the work is not completely defiladed. If it be necessary to defilade the interior from the part so cut off by the plane of site, the operation detailed in art 21 must be performed: if unnecessary, then it is required only that the command of the work over the ground from which it is not defiladed shall be five feet; the depth of the line of site below the plane tangent to the same ground must therefore never exceed three feet.

14. The inconvenience of being commanded by neighbouring heights does not always require to be removed by an increased relief; for it may easily be perceived that the natural plane of site of a proposed work might be such, that if produced it would pass

---

* The point of command is here considered to be the point of contact of the plane of sight with the ground, *not the highest point of the ground;* this latter being termed the point of culmination, or culminating point.

above all the higher ground in front of it. Though a commanding position is undoubtedly superior to a commanded one, yet if the rules of defilade have been properly applied in the construction of the fortifications, the defenders will find themselves as perfectly screened from the view of the enemy, in a fortress commanded by the surrounding ground, as if that fortress were constructed on a plain.

The following examples of the application of the principles of defilade to field-works will, it is presumed, be sufficient to render them perfectly intelligible.

To Defilade Open Works.

15. The most simple open works are the redan and the lunette. Let B C D, Fig. 71, be the plan of a redan, and A B C D E that of a lunette: the first operation is to fix the limits of the ground from which it is necessary to be defiladed.

We shall suppose that the boundary of these limits is, 1st, an arc of a circle described from the salient C with a radius of 300 yards; 2ndly, for the redan the lines B R and D S: for the lunette, the lines A K and E I, perpendicular to the extremities of the crests of the respective works, produced until they meet the arc previously described. The limit in height for the exterior space we shall here suppose to be *eight feet*, in order that the plane tangent to the exterior space, and parallel to the plane of defilade, may also be the plane of site. The second operation is to ascertain whether the commanding points are situated in front or in rear of the faces produced. By ground in front of face is understood that ground on which the face fires, and which lies on the same side of that face produced. By ground in rear of a face, is understood all the ground not comprised in the first definition within the limits of defilade before described. This distinction leads to the consideration of two different cases.

1st. When the commanding points are situated in front of the faces and flanks.

2nd. When those points are situated in rear of the same faces and flanks.

16. *Case* 1.—Let B C, C D. Fig. 79, be the plan of the crest of a redan. First, it is necessary to endeavour to regulate the relief of the crests so that they may be in the same plane of defilade; *i. e.* a plane passing eight feet above the exterior surface. In order to perform this operation, assume the height of any point O situated a little in rear of the gorge, and determine the plane of site as in art 12, selecting the plane which most nearly coincides with the surface of the ground on which the work is to be erected. From the distances of the points B, C, D, in the plane thus found, below the plane of comparison, subtract eight feet for the distances of the corresponding points of the crest below the latter plane.

17. If the conditions required by art. 13 are not fulfilled, then assume a distance for the point C, Fig. 80, below the plane of comparison, and find the points of contact of two tangents to the given surface, drawn in the direction of the faces B C and D C produced (Problem VIII.), and to which the point C is common. Graduate those tangents and find the scale of the plane containing them. This plane is called the *tangent plane*, and is here supposed to coincide with

the *plane of site*. The points B, C, and D in the plane of site should be higher than the surface of the ground next to them, but the difference of level should not exceed four feet.

Let *a b*, Fig. 80, be the plane of site, and suppose this plane to cut the given surface in the direction of the curve *g h i m n*, within the sector formed by the prolongations of the faces B C and D C. It is evident from an inspection of the figure, that the interior slopes cannot be seen from any part of the exterior space; it will then be sufficient to defilade each face from the ground in front of it; in order to do which, graduate the prolongations of the faces B C and D C, according to the given scale *a b*, and proceed to find the planes of sight as directed in Problem VII., art. 10. There will then be two scales of inclination for the planes of site; find their intersection C H, and also the intersection of those planes with the terreplein of the work. The position of these latter intersections with respect to C H will shew whether the natural plane of site can be taken, and, if not, to what extent it will be necessary to excavate the terreplein.

The method of proceeding above described is adapted to the case in which it is required to defilade a work already constructed, without increasing the relief.

18. Let A B C D E, Fig. 79, be the outline of a lunette, and suppose those five points are required to be placed in the same plane of defilade, and the plane of site is to be tangent to the exterior surface. As the plane of site ought to pass above all the ground in front of the line K I, we should first determine the

heights of the points A and E of the gorge, which points are projected on the line K I.

For this purpose, construct the section of the ground made by a vertical plane, of which the line K I is the horizontal trace, Prob. IV.; let $r\,a\,e\,v$ be this section, than any line $x\,y$ not more than four feet above it may be taken as the line of site; but it is in general more convenient to choose the line H T, a tangent in two points to the section $r\,a\,e\,v$; graduate the line K I to represent the line of site H T, and determine the plane of site, as in Problem VII.

19. *Case* 2.—First solution. Determine the relief of the crests B C, C D, Fig. 80, so that their prolongations may not intersect the exterior space (art. 17). Let $a\,b$ be the scale of the plane of site intersecting the ground in the direction of the curve $g\,h\,m\,i\,n$, contained within the sector formed by the prolongations of the faces B C and C D.

Find the planes of sight and of defilade of the faces B C and C D (art. 17), keeping the crest of each flank in the same plane as the adjoining face. The planes of site and defilade being parallel, and the divisions of their scales equal, they may both be represented on the same scale; it is only necessary to subtract eight feet from each number on the scale of the plane of site, to have the corresponding height of the plane of defilade; but as the numbers on the scale of the latter plane would then contain fractions, it is more convenient to mark a fresh set of points, where the whole numbers of that plane fall. If the relief of the flanks be regulated in the manner above mentioned, the interior slope of the flank A B will be covered by the face C D, and of the flank D E by the

Y

face B C, as far as the lines A D S, F B R. It then remains to determine whether the flanks cover each other from the view of the ground contained between the lines E R, A S, and the line K I, the boundary of the ground from which it is necessary to be defiladed. If this be not the case, then a traverse must be erected extending from the salient to the gorge of the work.

20. The relief of the flanks may also be thus regulated:—

Keep their lines of site in the same plane as those of the faces, then their interior slopes will be seen only by the portion of the exterior space $g\,h\,i\,m\,n$, cut off by the plane of site. In order to cover them from the view of this portion, two traverses are required.

Let B F, Fig. 80, be the direction of the crest of the traverse intended to defilade the flank A B. To determine its length, from the extremity of the flank A, draw A m tangent to the curve $g\,h$, &c., leaving all that curve in front of it; the point where the lines B F and A m intersect will be the extremity of the traverse, the height of which is to be found as in art. 21.

It may be remarked, that as the prolongation of the crest of the flank A B intersects the space $g\,h\,i\,m\,n$, it will be necessary to prolong the traverse on the parapet until it meets the line A $a\,o$. In whatever manner the relief of the flanks may be regulated, the terreplein in rear of them must always be determined by the two planes of sight previously found. The intersection of these planes with the ground should therefore be constructed. And unless they are in rear of the faces and flanks, it is a sufficient proof that the defilading operations have been incorrectly executed.

21. When this plane of site intersects the exterior surface in the direction of the curves $f\,g\,h\,i$, $a\,b\,c\,d\,e$, and $k\,l\,m\,n$, Fig. 81, the two latter curves, situated in rear of the faces produced, determine the new planes of site, as in art. 17; defilading each face from all the ground in front of it, and keeping the crest of each flank in the plane of defilade of the adjacent face.

In order to determine the form of the traverse required to protect the faces from reverse fire, find the scales of planes containing the lines B C and C D in the plane of site, and tangent to the ground in rear of those faces.

In graduating these scales subtract ten feet from each division, in order that the defilading plane of the traverse may pass two feet above the crests of the parapets; this height being required to protect the men mounted on the banquettes from reverse fire. These two scales will represent the planes of defilade required to determine the height of the traverse.

Let C F be the horizontal projection of the crest of the traverse, then that reverse plane of defilade which gives the greatest command for the traverse, is the plane required. The height at the point C being common to both the planes, it will only be necessary to compare the heights at the point F, in order to find which of the reverse planes is to be used. If the lines of site of B C and C D were in different planes, then the heights at the point C should also be compared, because the crests of the faces at that point would not then be on the same level; the traverse would, however, cause this inconvenience to disappear.

In constructing the work, the planes of site of the portions A B C F, F C D E, must be continued to the traverse; so that if C H were the intersection of those planes, it would be necessary to produce the plane of site of the portion A B C F, through the space contained within the triangle H C F; otherwise that part of the terreplein would not be properly defiladed.

If it were required to give the traverse the least possible relief, it should be constructed on the intersection of the planes of defilade.

22. It is necessary, in order to defilade completely the interior slopes, to continue the traverse up to the salient C; but this would render it impossible to place any defenders at the salient angle, which is always particularly desirable in field-works. To remedy this evil, the traverse is sometimes discontinued near the salient angle, as at the point L, and turned perpendicularly towards one of the faces. Another method of correcting this defect is to construct a bonnette extending from C to r, r. A bonnette is the name given to a parapet made higher at the salient angles than in other parts.

When the bonnette is only intended to protect the faces from enfilade fire, it should extend sufficiently far along each face to cover the banquette and its slope, or to cover the terreplein required for a piece of field artillery, and it should be made about one yard high.

23. *Second Solution.*—Let C F, Fig. 80, be the

direction of the crest of the traverse intended to cover the two terrepleins; find the heights of the point F in the planes of site of A B C F and F C D E.

Consider this point as lying in two planes, the one tangent to the ground in front of the flank A B and face B C, the other tangent to the ground in front of C D and D E.

These two planes will be the new planes of site for the two portions of the work, and consequently their intersections with a vertical at the point C should be on the same level.

The height of the traverse may be determined as in art. 21.

24. In treating of the mode of defilading open works, they have been supposed to be isolated; but it is necessary that they should be supported by troops in their rear, or be placed in such positions as may prevent their being turned.

In the first case, the vigour of the defence would greatly depend on the possibility of their garrisons being efficiently succoured.

Not only should the works therefore be defiladed, but also all the ground over which the troops destined to support them may be required to advance;—a condition difficult to fulfil, unless the ground itself afford cover for the troops when advancing from the principal works to the gorges of those in front.

TO DEFILADE ENCLOSED WORKS.

25. We will select, as an example, the most simple enclosed work—viz., a square redoubt. Three cases present themselves for consideration.

Case 1.—When the plane or planes of site do not intersect the exterior space, within the required limits.

This case occurs when the work is constructed on a plain, and in mountainous countries if the redoubt be placed on a height, or on an inclined surface, which, being prolonged towards the heights, passes above the commanding points, and on the side of the plain intersects the ground only at a great distance.

26. *Case* 2.—Let A B C D Fig. 82, be a square redoubt, to be constructed on a site commanded by the surrounding ground. The relief of the crests should be so regulated (art. 17) that the prolongations of the plane of site may not intersect the exterior space.

But it generally happens that the plane or planes of site intersect the surface of the earth, and this cannot occur without exposing two or more faces of the redoubt to be seen in reverse.

Let *a b c d* be the intersection of the plane of site with the ground; the faces A D and D C being seen in reverse, a traverse or parados must be erected in the direction A C. To defilade the part A B C, determine separately the planes of site for the faces A B and B C with reference only to the ground in front of them (art. 17).

The part A D C will also have its planes of site determined so as not to intersect the ground in front of those faces. The traverse should be discontinued near the salients A and C (art. 22).

To determine its height. Let the line D *s t* or D *p* be in the direction which appears to require the greatest relief for the traverse; find the point of contact of a tangent to the given surface drawn in the direction of one of the lines D s t or D p; graduate that tangent, and place the crest of the traverse in a parallel plane ten feet above it, or above a tangent drawn from B to ƒ, if that line is highest at s.

27. Let a b c d, e f g h, be the projections of two intersections of the planes of site with the exterior surface: all the faces of the redoubt would then be seen in reverse, if there were no traverse, but the traverse A C will cover them from reverse fire. It is necessary, in this case, to repeat the operations detailed in the preceding article, in order to determine the height of the traverse required to cover the faces A B and B C; and that tangent is to be used for the construction which gives the greatest relief for the traverse. The plane of site will be determined for each face as in the last article.

28. Sometimes the following more simple plan may be resorted to:—When the redoubt has a very evident command over the ground contained in the sectors M A T and P C Q, and the points of command are situated within the sectors N B O and S D R, determine the relief of the points A and C only; find the line of site corresponding to those points, and consider it as being common to both parts of the redoubt separated by the traverse.

29. If the planes of site intersect the ground in all the sectors formed by the prolongations of the faces, or in three only, it will be necessary to construct a traverse in the form of a cross in the direction of the diagonals of the redoubt.

30. Let m n o p, Fig. 83, be the intersection of the

plane of site with the ground; the faces A D, B C, and D C, will be seen in reverse.

The first may be covered by the traverses A E and B F, the last by the parados G H, the ends of the traverses and parados being extended one yard beyond the points E, F, G, and H, for greater security.

The terreplein of the part A E G H F B C D will be in the plane of site of A D, D C, and C B, because that plane does not intersect the ground in front of those places: the terreplein of the remaining space A B F H G E will be kept in a plane containing the line of site of A B, and tangent to the ground in front of that face. There will then necessarily be breaks in the terreplein, in the directions G E and H F.

The position of the parados should be such that this difference of level may not exceed one yard.

If the relief of the traverses B F and A E were required to be very great, in order to defilade the faces B C and A D, those faces may be defiladed in portions; a sufficient relief being given to the traverses B F, bf, to cover the parts B b and b C; A E, and ae covering in like manner A a and a D.

31. *Case* 3.—When the lines of site intersect the ground in the direction of the prolongations of the faces.

This cannot always be avoided; for, suppose that it is required to construct a redoubt on a plain in front of a hill, the crest of which is represented by the line X Y, Figs. 82 and 8 3, one of the salients may be turned towards the hill, as in Fig. 82, or one of the faces, Fig. 83. In the first case, all the prolongations will intersect the hill; and all the faces will be seen by reverse fire. In the second case, two prolongations only intersect the hill; one face is seen in reverse, and two are enfiladed: while one can neither be seen in reverse, nor enfiladed. If, then, it were necessary to trace the work in the first manner, the angles A and C should be made as small as possible, in order to diminish the length B D; if traced in the second manner, the faces A D and B C should for a similar reason, be made short.

The difficulties of defilading works of all descriptions may, and ought to be, met as much as possible by modifications of the outline. In some cases the whole of the face of a work cannot be defiladed by using a single plane, and here the ingenuity of the engineer will be exhibited by tracing his work so as to preserve as much direct defence as may be required, and to render the steps or traverses he may be obliged to construct available for the active as well as passive defence.

NOTE II.

To find the content of the frustrum of a cone, Fig. 127.

Given $BC = a$
$BE = l$
$EF = c.$

Let $EG = x$. Then $a : c :: l + x : x$,
and $a - c : c :: l + x - x : x :: l : x$
$$x(a - c) = cl$$
$$x = \frac{cl}{a - c} = \text{height of cone cut off.}$$

The content of the frustrum will be equal to the content of the whole cone minus the cone cut off.

To find the content of the whole cone, let p equal the ratio of the circumference of a circle to its diameter (π).

Then $\dfrac{pa^2}{3}\left(l + \dfrac{cl}{a-c}\right) =$ content of cone;

viz. $\dfrac{pa^2}{3}\left(\dfrac{al + cl - cl}{a-c}\right) =$ content of cone.

or, $\dfrac{pa^2}{3}\left(\dfrac{al}{a-c}\right)$.

The content of the cone cut off is $= \dfrac{pc^2}{3}\left(\dfrac{cl}{a-c}\right)$.

The content of any frustrum of a cone of which the radii of the circular ends and heights are known, is therefore equal to

$$\frac{pa^3l - pc^3l}{3(a-c)} = \frac{pl}{3(a-c)}(a^3 - c^3),$$

which, effecting the algebraical division, gives

$$\frac{pl}{3}(a^2 + ac + c^2).$$

To find the content of the crater of a common mine, we have $a = l$, and $c = \dfrac{l}{2}$; which values being substituted in the general expression, we shall have $\dfrac{pl}{3}\left(\dfrac{7l^2}{4}\right) = \dfrac{7pl^3}{12}$. But p is $= \dfrac{22}{7}$; therefore, $\dfrac{7pl^3}{12} = \dfrac{7}{12} \times \dfrac{22}{7} l^3 = \dfrac{11}{6} l^3$; viz. the content of the crater is equal to $\dfrac{11}{6}$ of the cube of the line of least resistance.

NOTE III.

Let us suppose that a horizontal gallery has its superior surface placed at the distance d, below the horizontal plane passing through the centre of the mine, and its side sheeting at a distance c, from the vertical plane passing through the same centre; if from this centre a perpendicular be let fall on the edge of the gallery nearest to the charge, the rupture will extend on each side of the perpendicular to a distance represented by

$$\sqrt{\left(\frac{19}{16}l^2 - \frac{49}{32}d^2\right)} - c.$$

For let A B H, Fig. 128, be the ellipsoid of rupture, then we have,

Given $AC = a = \frac{7}{4}l$ $CE = c$
$CB = b = l\sqrt{2}$ $CB = d,$

to find D H and C H, &c.

From H erect H I perpendicular to the transverse axis and let C I $=x$.

Then $a^2:b^2::\overline{a+x}.\overline{a-x}:d^2$
$$a^2d^2 = a^2b^2 - b^2x^2$$
$$x^2 = \frac{a^2b^2 - a^2d^2}{b^2} = \frac{a^2(b^2 - d^2)}{b^2}$$
$$x = a\sqrt{\frac{(b^2 - d^2)}{b^2}} = a\sqrt{1 - \frac{d^2}{b^2}};$$
but $DH = x - c = a\sqrt{1 - \frac{d^2}{b^2}} - c.$

In which expression, substituting the known values of a and b, we get

$$DH = \sqrt{\left(\frac{49}{16}l^2 - \frac{49}{32}d^2\right)} - c.$$

The length of gallery destroyed will therefore be equal to double this distance, and the sub-horizontal radius of rupture with respect to the gallery will be represented by

$$\sqrt{\tfrac{49}{16}l^2 - \tfrac{17}{32}d^2};$$

For $FH = c + DH = \sqrt{\tfrac{49}{16}l^2 - \tfrac{49}{32}d^2}$

$CH^2 = FH^2 + FC^2 = \tfrac{49}{16}l^2 - \tfrac{49}{32}d^2 + d^2$

$CH = \sqrt{\tfrac{49}{16}l^2 - \tfrac{17}{32}d^2}.$

Suppose, now, a vertical shaft at the distance c from the centre of the charge, the extent of the shaft destroyed by the explosion of the mine will be represented by

$$2\sqrt{\frac{(98l^2 - 32c^2)}{7}}$$

for, let A E I H Fig. 129 be the ellipsoid of rupture, we then have given

$AC = a = \tfrac{7}{4}l,$ $CE = b = l\sqrt{2},$
$CD = c$: required HI and CH.

Let $BH = x$. Then $a^2 : b^2 :: \overline{a+c} \cdot \overline{a-c} : x^2$

$x^2 a^2 = b^2 a^2 - b^2 c^2$

$x = \sqrt{\dfrac{b^2(a^2 - c^2)}{a^2}} = \sqrt{1 - \dfrac{c^2}{a^2}}$

Therefore, $HI = 2b\sqrt{1 - \dfrac{c^2}{a^2}}$; or, substituting the values of a and b,

$$HI = 2\sqrt{2l^2 - \tfrac{32c^2}{49}} \text{ or } \frac{2\sqrt{98l^2 - 32c^2}}{7}.$$

The distance of the charge from each of the extremities of the broken part, viz., the sub-horizontal radius of rupture, with respect to the shaft, will be

NOTE III. 333

$$\sqrt{\frac{(98l^2 + 17c^2)}{7}}$$

for $CH = \sqrt{c^2 + x^2} = \sqrt{c^2 + b - \frac{b^2c^2}{a^2}}$;

or substituting values of *a* and *b*.

$$CH = \sqrt{\frac{17}{49}c^2 + 2l^2} \text{ or } \frac{\sqrt{(98l^2 + 17c^2)}}{7}.$$

In general, let *r* be the radius of rupture in the direction formed by the angle ϕ and a vertical line passing through the centre of the charge; then

$$r = \frac{7}{4}l\sqrt{\left(\frac{1 + \tan^2\phi}{\tan^2\phi + \frac{49}{32}}\right)};$$

For in Fig. 130, given $AC = a = \frac{7}{4}l$,

$CB = b = l\sqrt{2}$, angle $HCF = \phi$,

to find CF.

Put $FE = y$; then $CF = y . \sec\phi$.

Therefore, $CE = \sqrt{(y^2\sec^2\phi - y^2)}$.

But $a^2 : b^2 :: \overline{a + CE} \times \overline{a - CE} : y^2$

$a^2 : b^2 :: a^2 - y^2\sec^2\phi + y^2 : y^2$

$a^2y^2 = a^2b^2 - b^2y^2\sec^2\phi + b^2y^2$

$a^2b^2 = (a^2 + b^2\sec^2\phi - b^2)y^2$

$$y^2 = \frac{a^2b^2}{a^2 + b^2\sec^2\phi - b^2}$$

$$y = \frac{ab}{\sqrt{(a^2 + b^2\sec^2\phi - b^2)}} = ab\sqrt{\left(\frac{1}{a^2 + b^2\sec^2\phi - b^2}\right)}$$

But $\sec^2\phi = 1 + \tan^2\phi$.

Therefore, $\sec\phi = \sqrt{1 + \tan^2\phi}$

Substituting the value of $\sec^2\phi$ in the value of *y* we get

$$y = ab\sqrt{\left(\frac{1}{a^2 + b^2\tan^2\phi}\right)}$$

But $CF = y . \sec\phi$.

Therefore, $CF = ab\sqrt{\left(\dfrac{1+\tan^2\phi}{a^2+b^2\tan^2\phi}\right)}$, and substituting in this equation the known values of a and b.

$$CF = \frac{7}{4}l\cdot\sqrt{2}\sqrt{\left(\dfrac{1+\tan^2\phi}{\frac{49}{16}l^2+2l^2\tan^2\phi}\right)}$$

$$= \frac{7}{4}l\sqrt{\left(\dfrac{2+2\tan^2\phi}{l^2(\frac{49}{16}+2\tan^2\phi)}\right)}$$

$$= \frac{7}{4}l\sqrt{\left(\dfrac{1+\tan^2\phi}{\frac{49}{32}+\tan^2\phi}\right)}.$$

NOTE IV.

Great difference of opinion has existed among miners as to what should be the charge of a "globe of compression." The following method of considering this subject appears to be as little open to objection as any other that has yet been devised.

One of the globes of compression at the siege of Schweidnitz was charged with 4600 lbs. of powder, which being placed under a line of least resistance of 10 feet, produced a crater of $41\frac{1}{2}$ feet radius.

Let us suppose that the globe of compression in question was exploded in common earth, and ascertain under what line of least resistance the same charge of 4600 lbs. must be placed in order to produce the effect of a common mine, viz., a crater of a radius equal to the length of the line of least resistance. Now, as the charges of common mines are in proportion to the cubes of their lines of least resistance, we have

$$100 \text{ lbs.} : 10^3 :: 46,000 \text{ lbs.} : 4600 ;$$

and, extracting the root, we find 36 feet nearly to be the line of least resistance sought.

NOTE IV. 335

In Fig. 131 are represented the effects of the globe of compression exploded at Schweidnitz, and of a common mine under the same line of least resistance; their difference being divided into three equal parts; and also the crater of a common mine under a similar line of least resistance, viz., 16 feet, and under the line of least resistance corresponding to the charge of 4600 lbs.: the difference between these two craters being, in like manner, divided into three equal parts.

It appears evident, that if under a line of least resistance of 16 feet we wish to produce craters of the radii A B, A C, we must use the charges corresponding to the lines of least resistance $a\,b$ and $a\,c$.

From the above reasoning it follows, that a rule to find the charge for a globe of compression may be thus determined:—

Subtract the given line of least resistance (16 feet) from the radius of the crater of the globe of compression (41½ feet), and also from the line of least resistance of the common mine requiring the same charge (36 feet); divide the latter difference by the former:

$$\text{we then have } \frac{20 \text{ ft.}}{25\tfrac{1}{4} \text{ ft.}} = \cdot 8.$$

The rule, therefore, is to "subtract the given line of least resistance from the radius of the crater to be produced; multiply the difference by ·8; and the product, added to the given line of least resistance, gives the line of least resistance of a common mine requiring the same charge as the globe of compression. This rule gives larger charges for the other globes of compression exploded at Schweidnitz than were actually used; the charges deduced from it are also greater than those found by Marescot's more complex rule: the error, therefore, if there be any, lies on the right side.

NOTE V.

Observing at one of Professor Faraday's Lectures, in 1834, the powerful action of the galvanic current on platinum wire, it occurred to me that this would furnish a certain mode of firing charges of powder under water. With the permission of the Professor, and Mr. Marsh's assistance, the following experiment was exhibited at the close of the lecture in the following week, before the Gentleman Cadets and several officers of the Royal Artillery and Royal Engineers, in the Chemical Lecture Room of the Royal Military Academy. Three wires, each about thirty feet long, were coiled in three tubs of water, secured at convenient distances to upright sticks, that the voltaic current might be made to pass through the entire length of the wires. The two ends of the wire coiled in the centre tub were then brought out of the water, and connected with the wires in the other two tubs, by means of a short piece of platinum wire, passed through a cartridge of powder; one wire was then connected with the pole of a voltaic battery, and having explained the object of my experiment, I completed the circuit by uniting the other extreme wire with the opposite pole, but no explosion took place. The reason of this failure immediately suggested itself to Professor Faraday; it was, that none of the very fine platinum wire being in the laboratory, a heavier description of wire had been used. An additional battery was therefore immediately added, and the voltaic current being again completed, an instantaneous explosion of both charges of powder took place; demonstrating the practicability of exploding charges under water, with the most perfect certainty, by the voltaic action on platinum wire; provided a sufficiently fine platinum, or iron, wire is used to check the voltaic current, which would otherwise pass without sufficiently heating the connecting wires to fire the powder, as occurred in the first instance, in the above-mentioned experiment. This mode of firing charges under water has since been extensively employed without the occurrence of a single failure.

I. S. MACAULAY.

THE END.

LONDON:
G. J. PALMER, 27, LAMBS CONDUIT STREET.

www.ingramcontent.com/pod-product-compliance
Lightning Source LLC
Chambersburg PA
CBHW030322240426
43673CB00040B/1246